SIGHT READING SUCCESS

A Daily Workout for Developing Confident Choirs

By Stan McGill and Morris Stevens

Online Exercises and audio files for this book are stored in your Hal Leonard My Library account and may be viewed/streamed from that location or downloaded to your computer.

Log on to www.halleonard.com/mylibrary and enter the unique code below.

Once you have set up your secure account, you may access these files at any time and from any device connected to the internet.

To access Media files, go to:
www.halleonard.com/mylibrary

Enter Code
4779-8925-6932-9585

ISBN 978-1-49-509632-4

7777 W. Bluemound Rd. P.O. Box 13819 Milwaukee, WI 53213

In Australia Contact:
Hal Leonard Australia Pty. Ltd.
4 Lentara Court
Cheltenham, Victoria, 3192 Australia
Email: ausadmin@halleonard.com.au

Visit Hal Leonard Online at
www.halleonard.com

TABLE OF CONTENTS

INTRODUCTION

This choral sight reading resource is designed to help secondary choir students improve their music literacy. There are several sight reading systems that may be used: moveable do solfège, fixed do solfège, numbers and perhaps others. It is our hope that with daily use, this book will help your choir build confidence and sharpen music literacy skills. All exercises are original and gradually progress in the level of challenge. The "helpful hints" are compilations of over sixty years of successful secondary choral teaching by the authors.

HOW TO USE THIS BOOK

This SSA sight reading methods book is designed to prepare secondary choirs for sight reading contests through daily practice. The book is a 5 month project, containing 140 SSA exercises in various keys and time signatures:

Month 1: Two 2 measure exercises daily (40 exercises)

Month 2: Two 4 measure exercises daily (40 exercises)

Month 3: One 8 measure exercise daily (20 exercises)

Month 4: One 16 measure exercise daily (20 exercises)

Month 5: One 32 measure exercise daily (20 exercises)

Though the words "sight reading" are used to describe this method, directors and choirs should consider it as a tool to improve music literacy. There is great benefit in repeating exercises and developing skills. If used on a regular basis, choirs will improve:

- Interval recognition by sound and sight
- Rhythmic and metric skills
- Choral balance and blend
- Independent, sectional and choral literacy skills
- Dynamic and articulation recognition and implementation
- Altered pitches
- Major/minor key modulations
- Consonant and dissonant choral chords

AUDIO FILES

Audio files are included in My Library as a resource for reviewing the exercises or a practice tool for students. They may be streamed from the site or downloaded to your computer.

HELPFUL HINTS

- Know your choir section by section. Realize the strengths and weaknesses of every section and within each section.
- Routinely work to improve your choir's sight reading skills.
- As suggested by Harold Hill in *The Music Man*, use the "think system." Develop a strong line of communication, both verbal and visual, between director and choir.
- Select music for your choir they can read, yet is challenging enough to stretch their sight reading skills.
- Establish a routine with your sight reading time. Help the choir become comfortable and confident with the sight reading process.
- If you are preparing your choir for a sight reading contest, be familiar with the rules and practice procedures. Be aware of do's and don'ts for director as well as choir.
- Spend time determining a workable sight reading standing formation. Place your stronger readers in strategic places within the section. Likewise, give thought to where each section should stand.
- Don't over-conduct. Conducting gestures should be made when you most want the choir's attention. The less you direct, the more responsibility you place on each singer and the choir.
- Use conducting gestures highlighting the actual rhythmic structure of the phrase.
- Learn to read vertically as well as horizontally.
- With the more advanced reading choir, venture to be as musical as possible. Phrasing will not only make for a more musical performance, it will actually help unify the choral sound.
- Eye contact with your choir is important for communication as well as developing confidence with your singers.
- Be positive, yet honest.
- Be certain to end every sight reading experience with your choir by sharing a realistic but encouraging analysis of their reading.
- Keep tempos slow and the pulse strong and steady.
- Hold every student accountable and involved, even the weakest readers.
- Standing rather than sitting helps your choir be more alert as well as establishes a better posture for singing.
- Anticipate problems before they occur.
- Locate potential trouble spots and discuss issues before initial singing.
- Use discussion time wisely. Spend time on challenging rhythms, staggered entrances, isolated/exposed spots, key changes, meter changes, altered pitches, page turns and other places of concern.
- Set tempo for the quickest rhythms of the piece to be comfortably sung, allowing you and choir to look ahead. Optimum sight-reading tempo is circa 50-55 bpm.

2-MEASURE EXERCISES

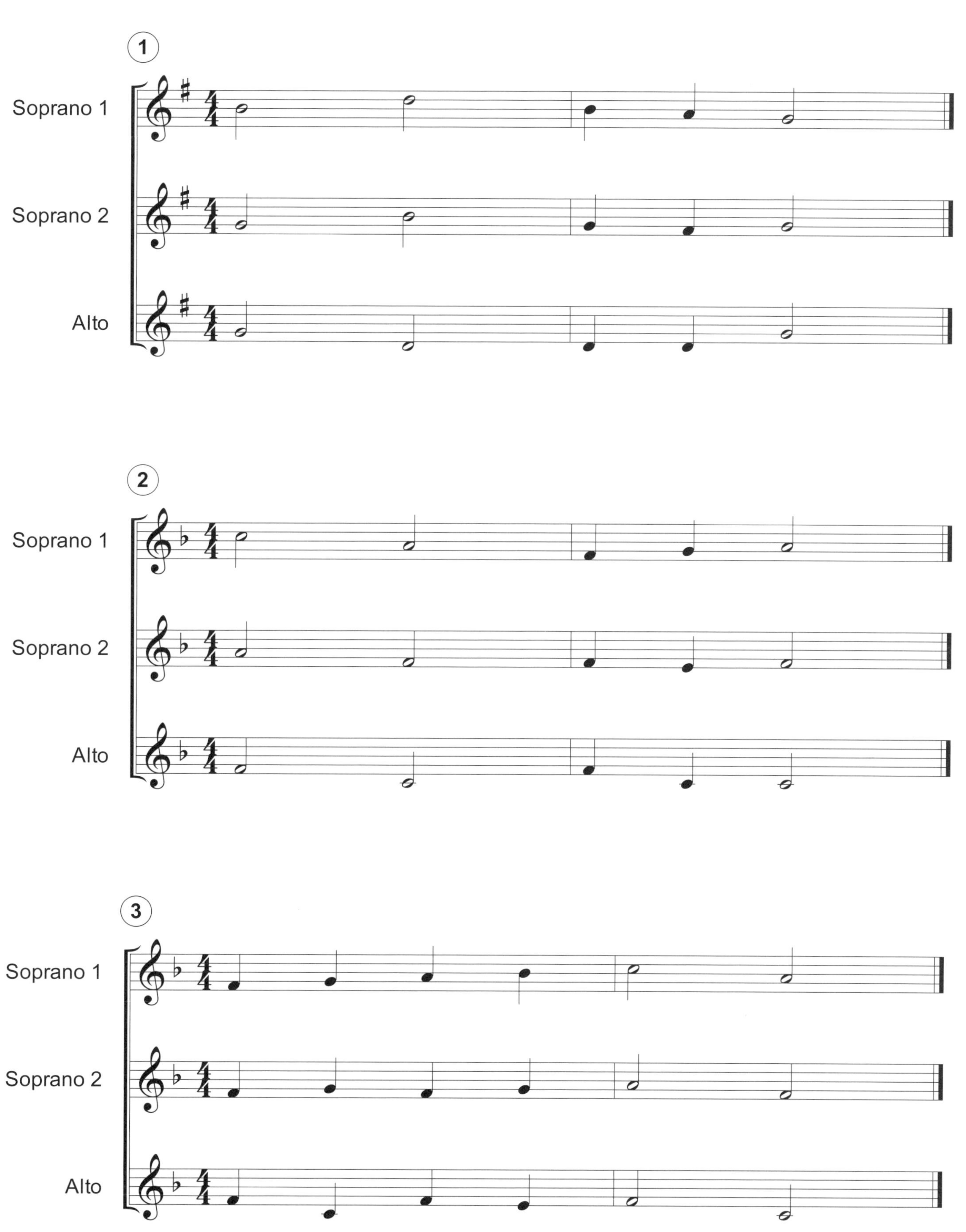

4
Soprano 1
Soprano 2
Alto
5
Soprano 1
Soprano 2
Alto
6
Soprano 1
Soprano 2
Alto

7
Soprano 1
Soprano 2
Alto
8
Soprano 1
Soprano 2
Alto
9
Soprano 1
Soprano 2
Alto

10
Soprano 1
Soprano 2
Alto
11
Soprano 1
Soprano 2
Alto
12
Soprano 1
Soprano 2
Alto

13
Soprano 1
Soprano 2
Alto
14
Soprano 1
Soprano 2
Alto
15
Soprano 1
Soprano 2
Alto

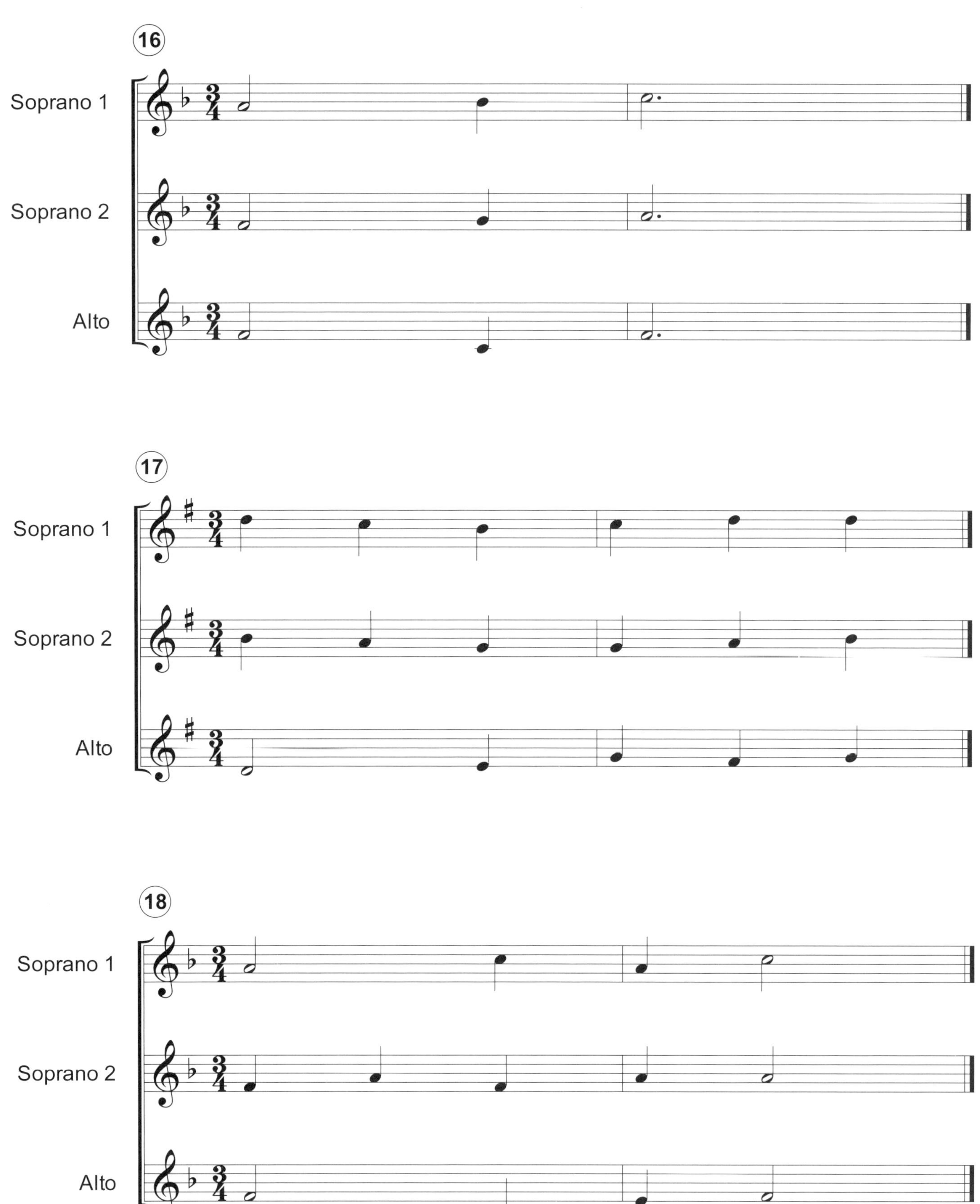
16
Soprano 1
Soprano 2
Alto
17
Soprano 1
Soprano 2
Alto
18
Soprano 1
Soprano 2
Alto

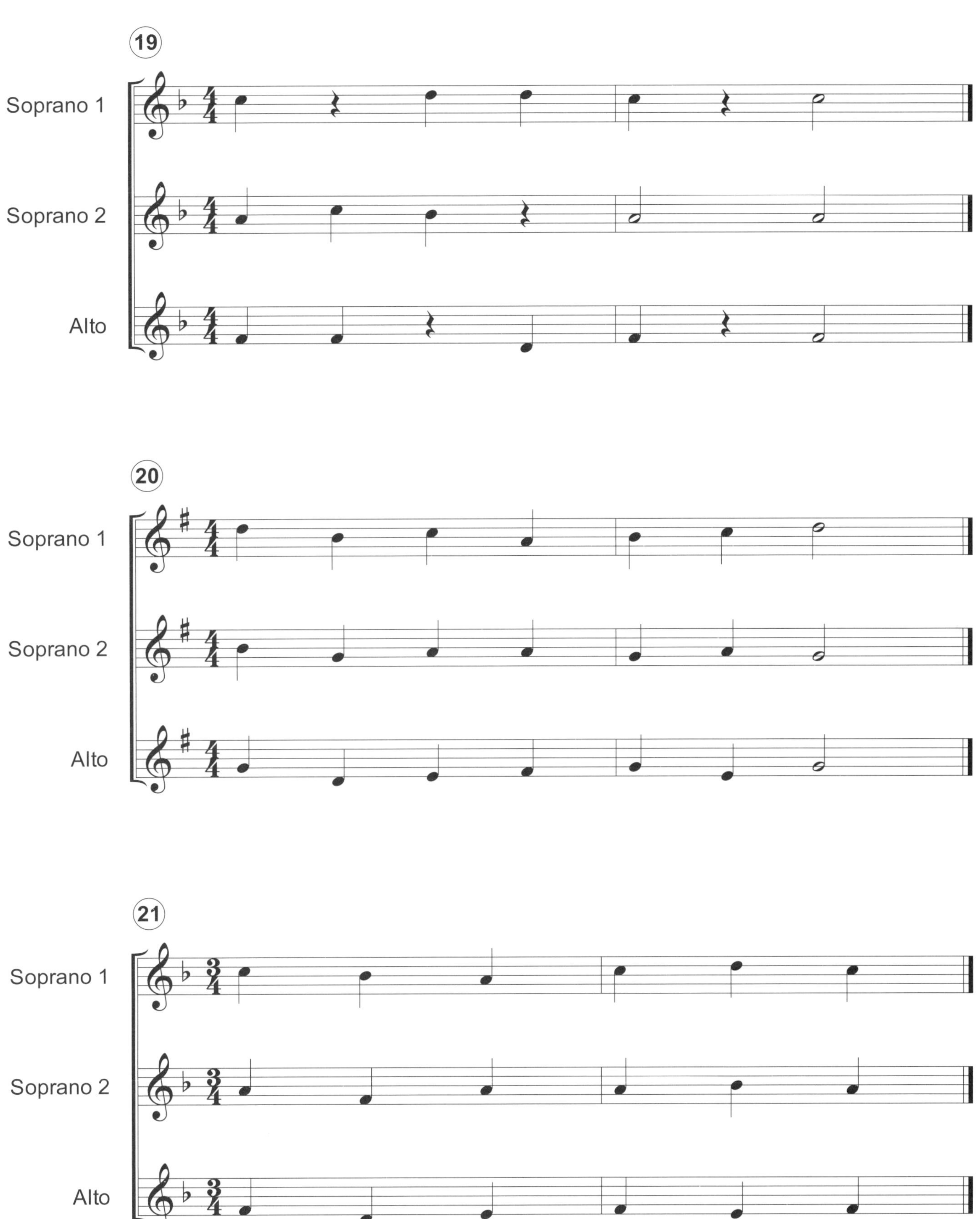
19
Soprano 1
Soprano 2
Alto
20
Soprano 1
Soprano 2
Alto
21
Soprano 1
Soprano 2
Alto

22
Soprano 1
Soprano 2
Alto
23
Soprano 1
Soprano 2
Alto
24
Soprano 1
Soprano 2
Alto

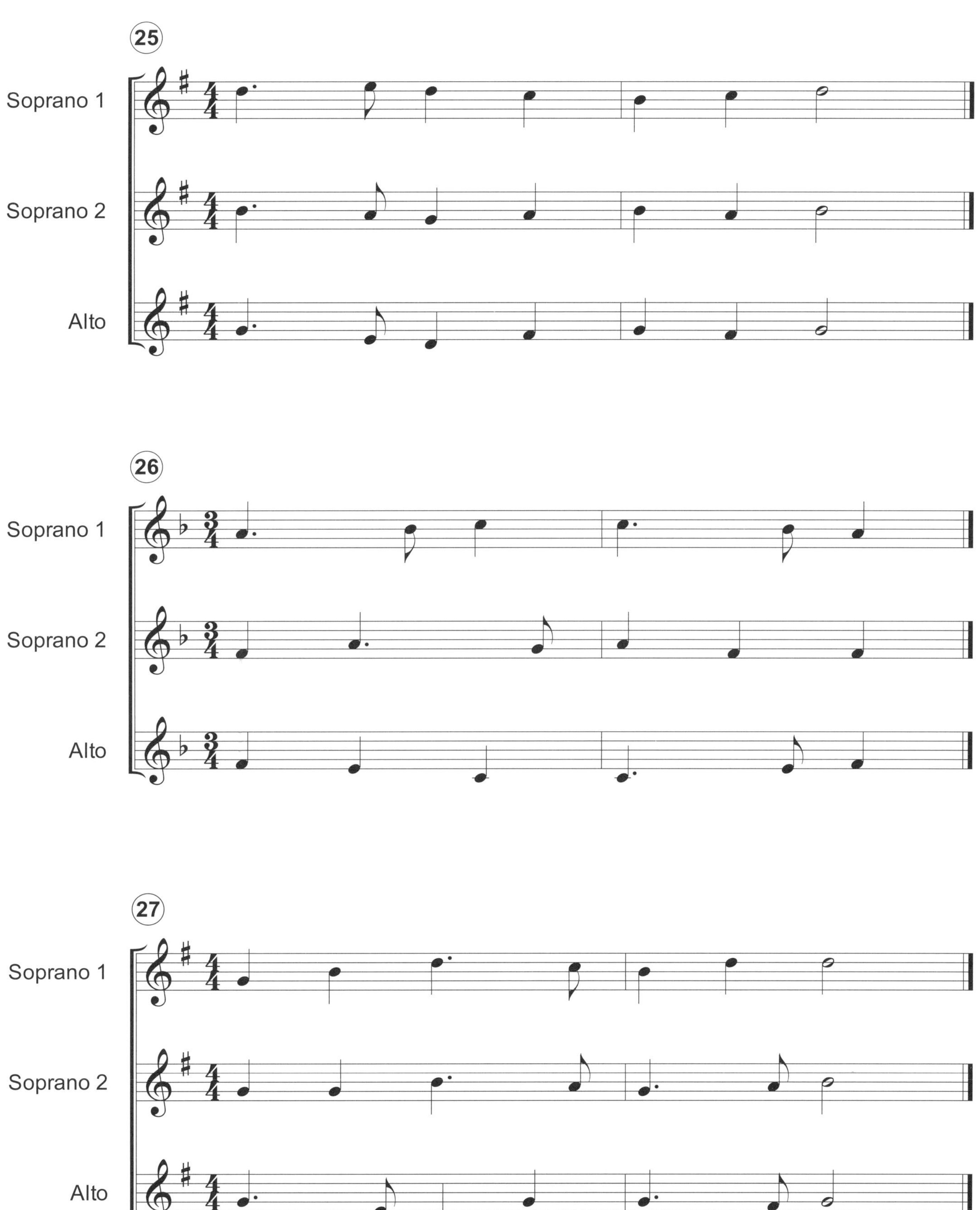
25
Soprano 1
Soprano 2
Alto
26
Soprano 1
Soprano 2
Alto
27
Soprano 1
Soprano 2
Alto

28
Soprano 1
Soprano 2
Alto
29
Soprano 1
Soprano 2
Alto
30
Soprano 1
Soprano 2
Alto

31
Soprano 1
Soprano 2
Alto
32
Soprano 1
Soprano 2
Alto
33
Soprano 1
Soprano 2
Alto

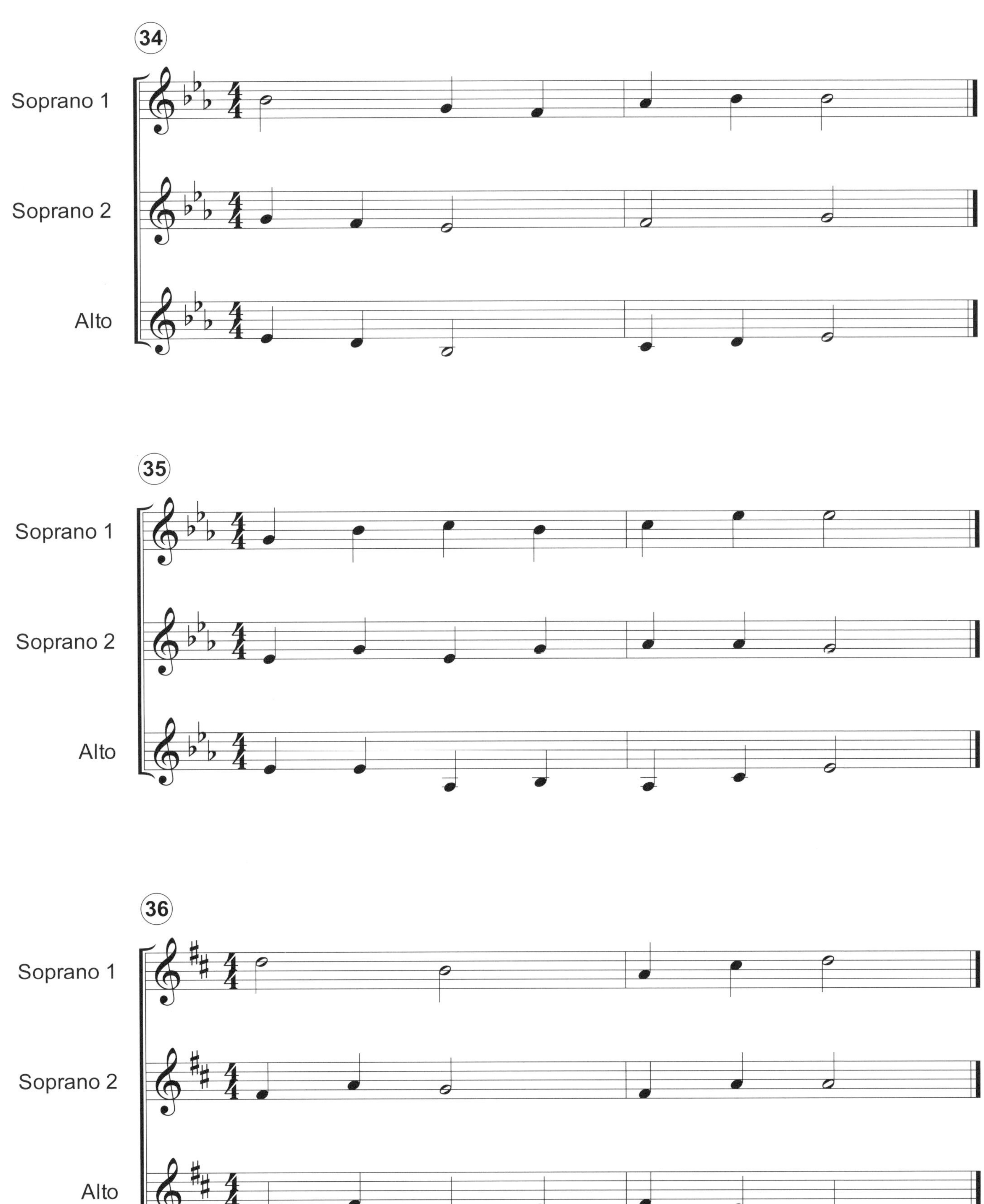
34
Soprano 1
Soprano 2
Alto
35
Soprano 1
Soprano 2
Alto
36
Soprano 1
Soprano 2
Alto

37
Soprano 1
Soprano 2
Alto
38
Soprano 1
Soprano 2
Alto
39
Soprano 1
Soprano 2
Alto

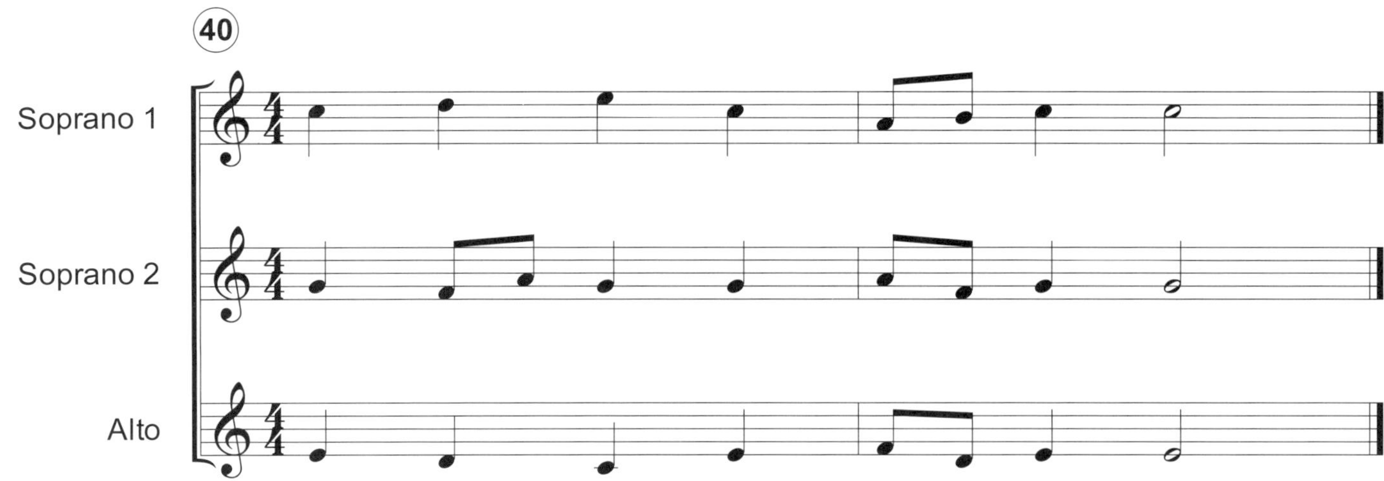
40
Soprano 1
Soprano 2
Alto

4-MEASURE EXERCISES

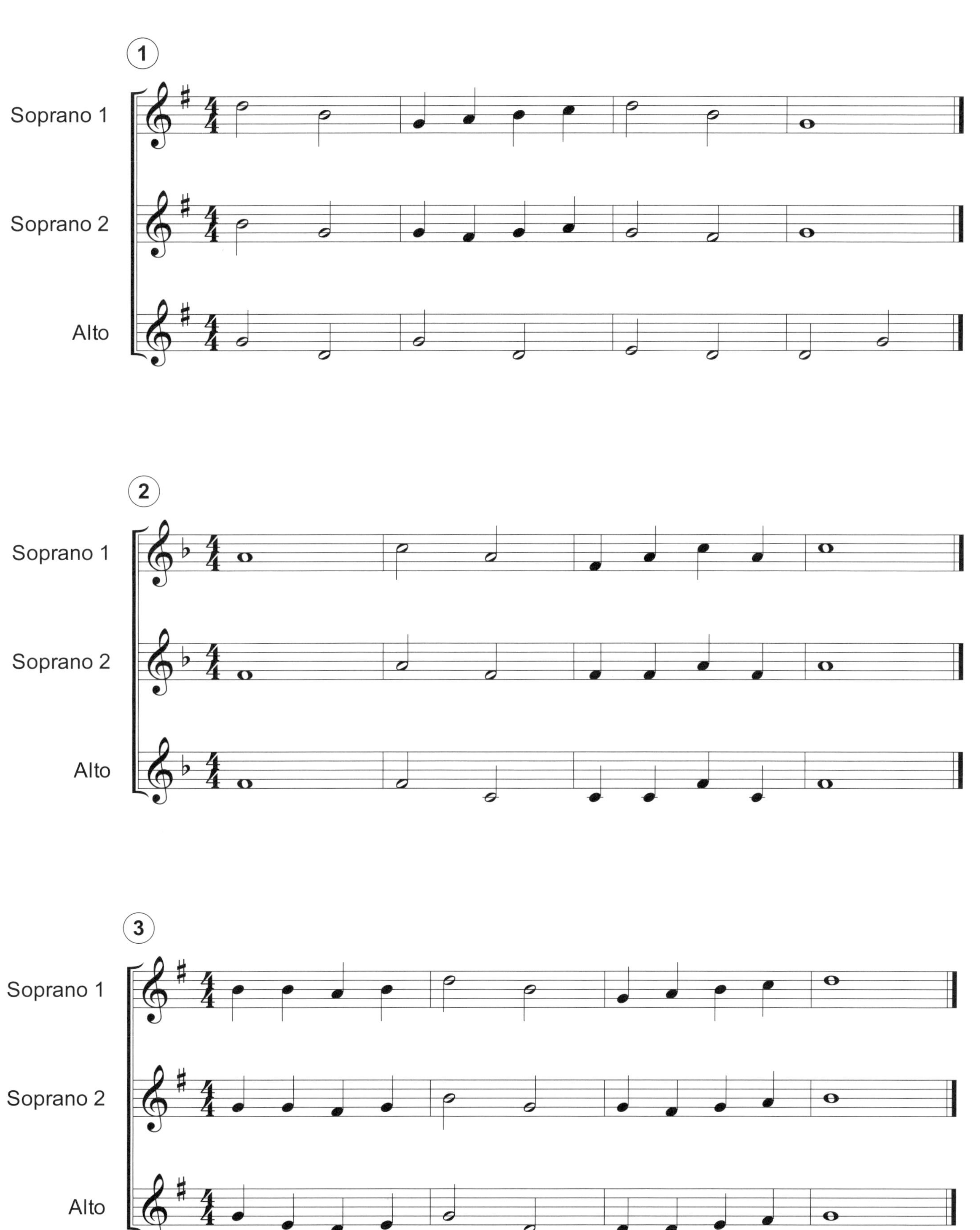

4
Soprano 1
Soprano 2
Alto

5
Soprano 1
Soprano 2
Alto

6
Soprano 1
Soprano 2
Alto

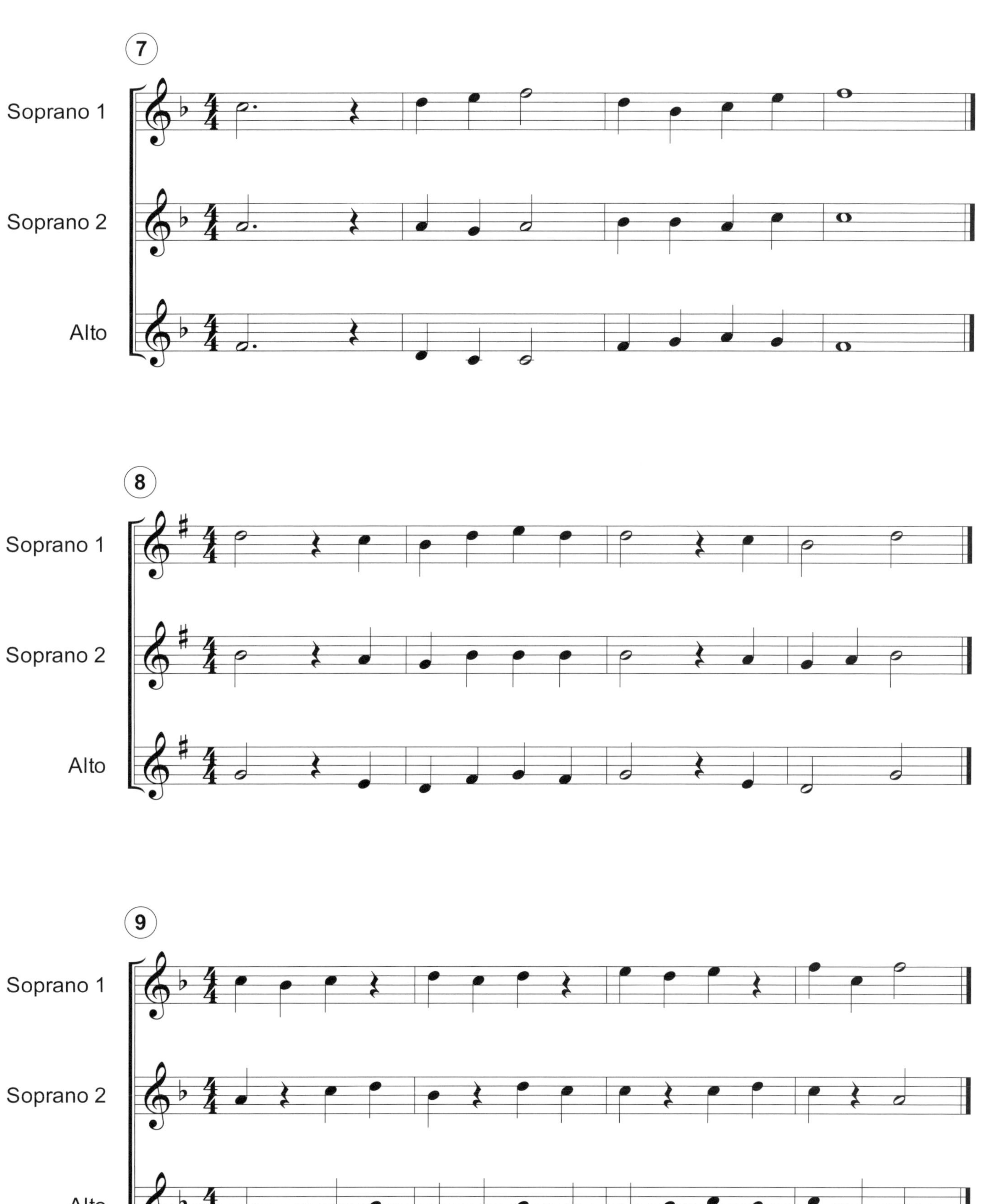
7
Soprano 1
Soprano 2
Alto
8
Soprano 1
Soprano 2
Alto
9
Soprano 1
Soprano 2
Alto

10

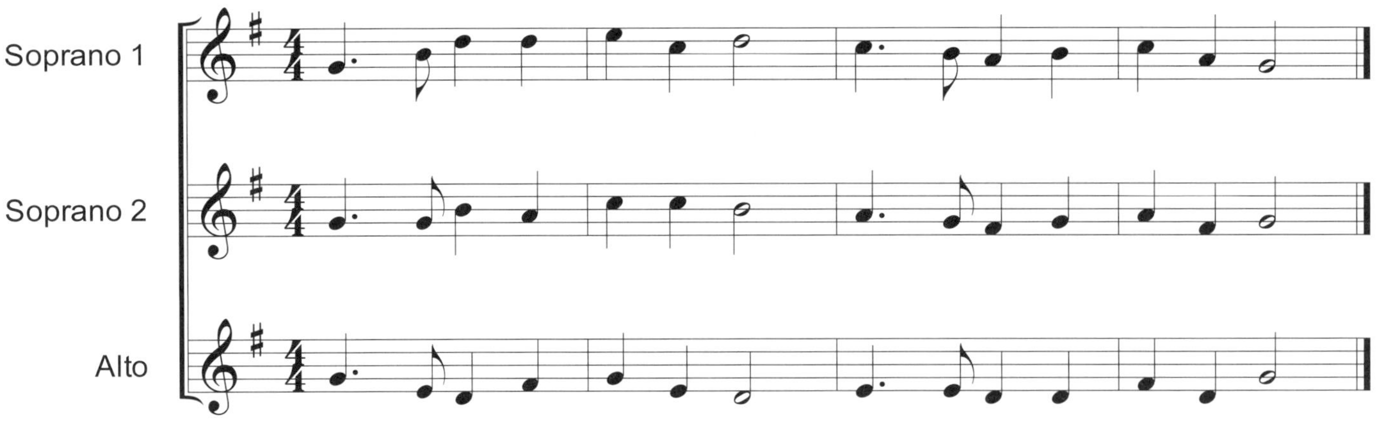
Soprano 1
Soprano 2
Alto

11

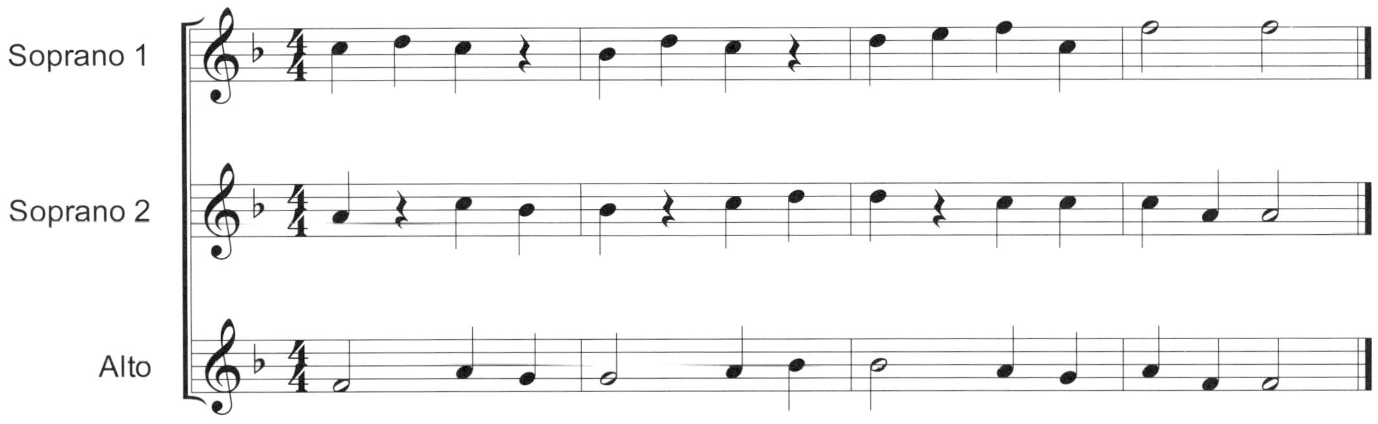
Soprano 1
Soprano 2
Alto

12

Soprano 1
Soprano 2
Alto

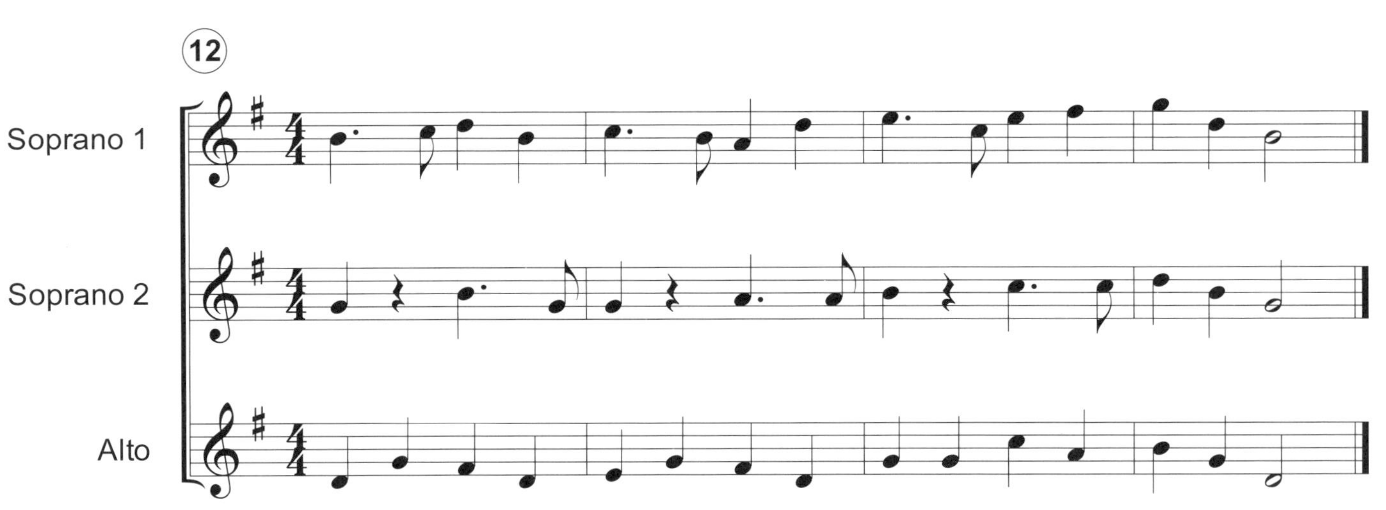

13
Soprano 1
Soprano 2
Alto
14
Soprano 1
Soprano 2
Alto
15
Soprano 1
Soprano 2
Alto

16
Soprano 1
Soprano 2
Alto
17
Soprano 1
Soprano 2
Alto
18
Soprano 1
Soprano 2
Alto

19
Soprano 1
Soprano 2
Alto
20
Soprano 1
Soprano 2
Alto
21
Soprano 1
Soprano 2
Alto

22
Soprano 1
Soprano 2
Alto
23
Soprano 1
Soprano 2
Alto
24
Soprano 1
Soprano 2
Alto

25
Soprano 1
Soprano 2
Alto
26
Soprano 1
Soprano 2
Alto
27
Soprano 1
Soprano 2
Alto

28

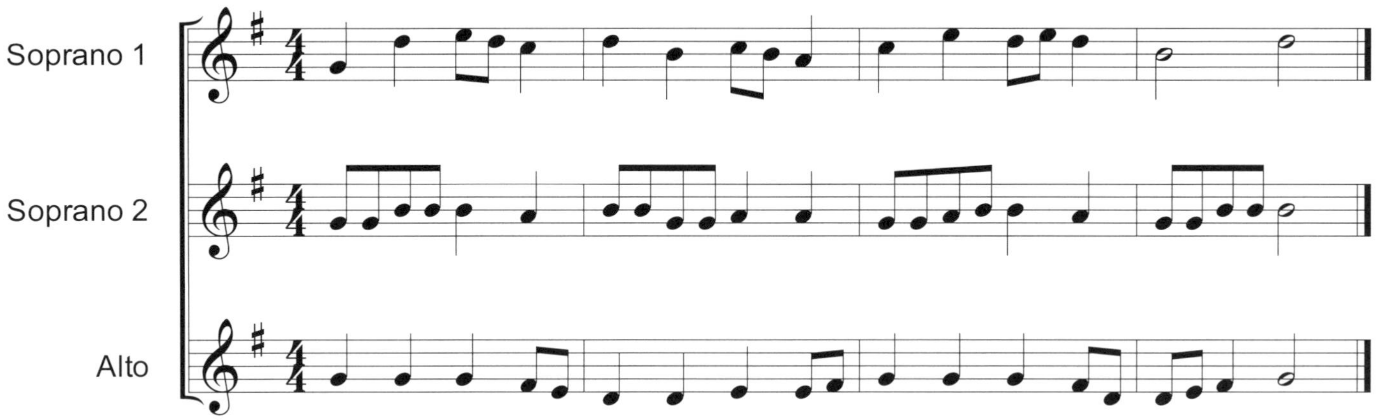
Soprano 1
Soprano 2
Alto

29

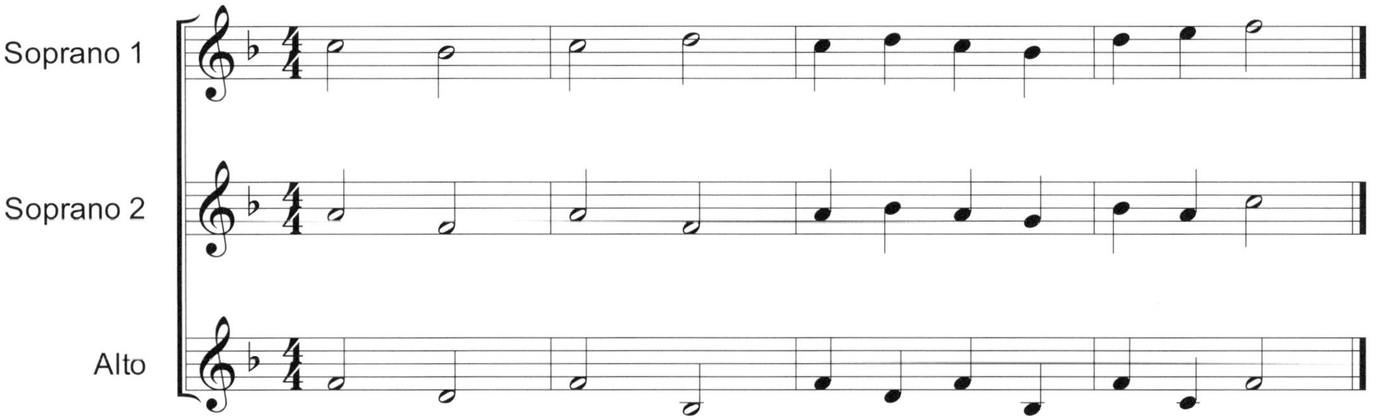
Soprano 1
Soprano 2
Alto

30

Soprano 1
Soprano 2
Alto

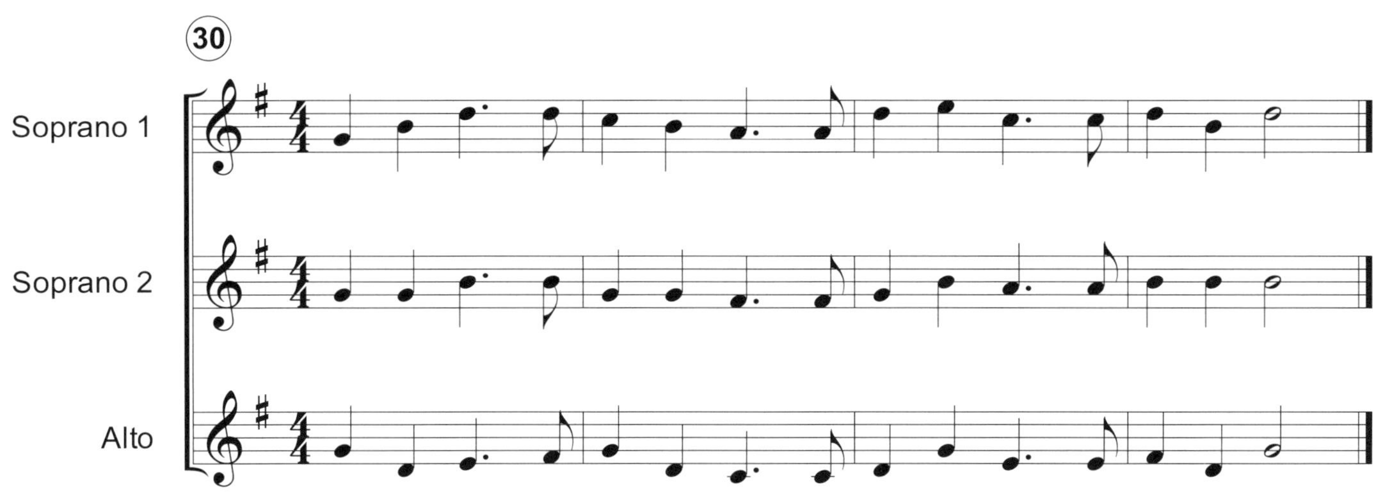

31
Soprano 1
Soprano 2
Alto
32
Soprano 1
Soprano 2
Alto
33
Soprano 1
Soprano 2
Alto

34
Soprano 1
Soprano 2
Alto
35
Soprano 1
Soprano 2
Alto
36
Soprano 1
Soprano 2
Alto

37
Soprano 1
Soprano 2
Alto
38
Soprano 1
Soprano 2
Alto
39
Soprano 1
Soprano 2
Alto

40
Soprano 1
Soprano 2
Alto

8-MEASURE EXERCISES

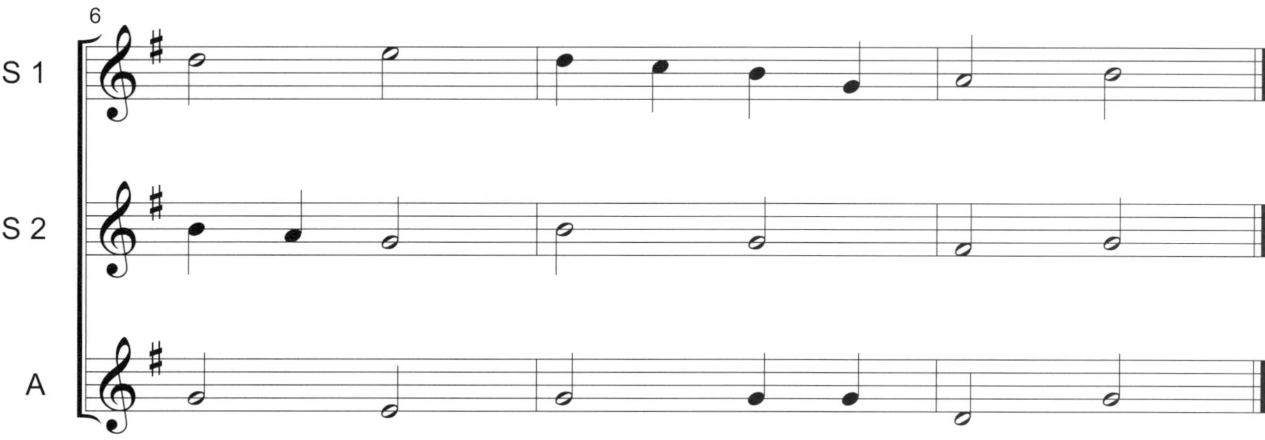

5
S 1
S 2
A

3
Soprano 1
Soprano 2
Alto

5
S 1
S 2
A

4
Soprano 1
Soprano 2
Alto

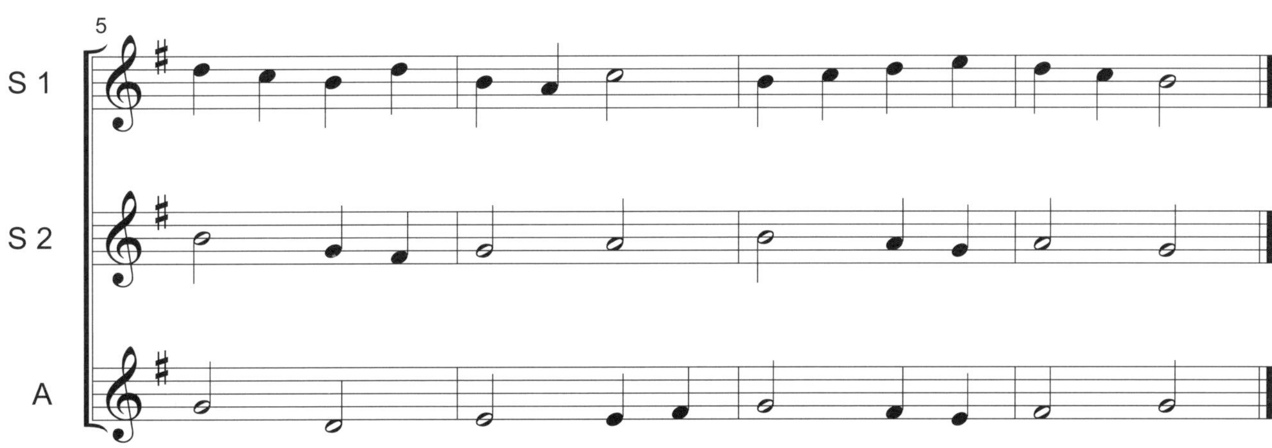
5
S 1
S 2
A

5
Soprano 1
Soprano 2
Alto

5
S 1
S 2
A

6
Soprano 1
Soprano 2
Alto

5
S 1
S 2
A

7
Soprano 1
Soprano 2
Alto

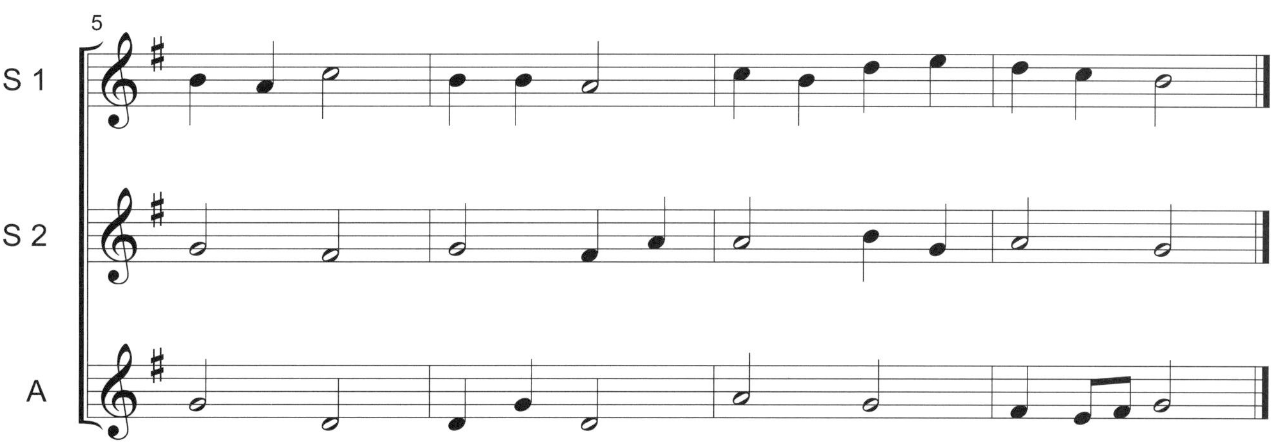
5
S 1
S 2
A

8
Soprano 1
Soprano 2
Alto

5
S 1
S 2
A

9
Soprano 1
Soprano 2
Alto

5
S 1
S 2
A

10
Soprano 1
Soprano 2
Alto
5
S 1
S 2
A
11
Soprano 1
Soprano 2
Alto

5
S 1
S 2
A

12
Soprano 1
Soprano 2
Alto

5
S 1
S 2
A

13
Soprano 1
Soprano 2
Alto
5
S 1
S 2
A
14
Soprano 1
Soprano 2
Alto

5
S 1
S 2
A

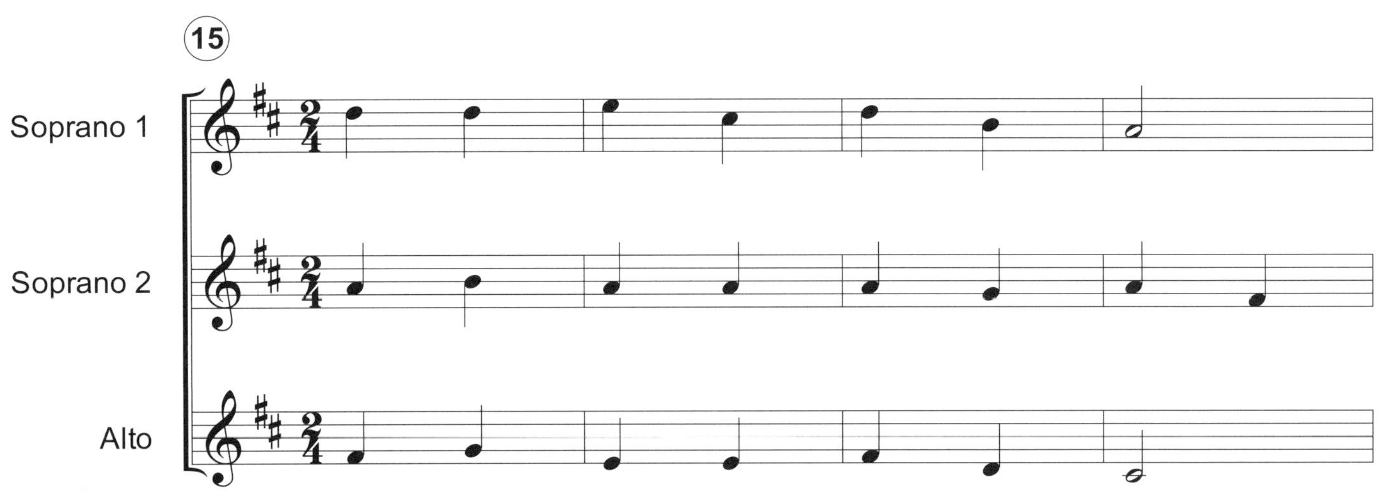
15
Soprano 1
Soprano 2
Alto

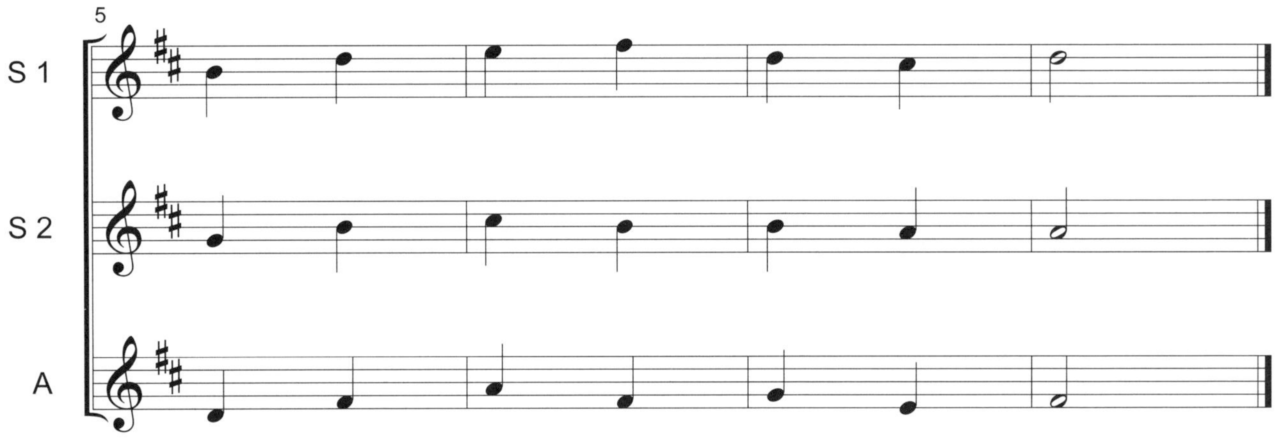
5
S 1
S 2
A

16
Soprano 1
Soprano 2
Alto
5
S 1
S 2
A
17
Soprano 1
Soprano 2
Alto

5
S 1
S 2
A
18
Soprano
Alto
Tenor
Bass
5
S
A
T
B

19
Soprano 1
Soprano 2
Alto
5
S 1
S 2
A
20
Soprano 1
Soprano 2
Alto

5
S 1
S 2
A

16-MEASURE EXERCISES

13
S 1
S 2
A

2
Soprano 1
Soprano 2
Alto

5
S 1
S 2
A

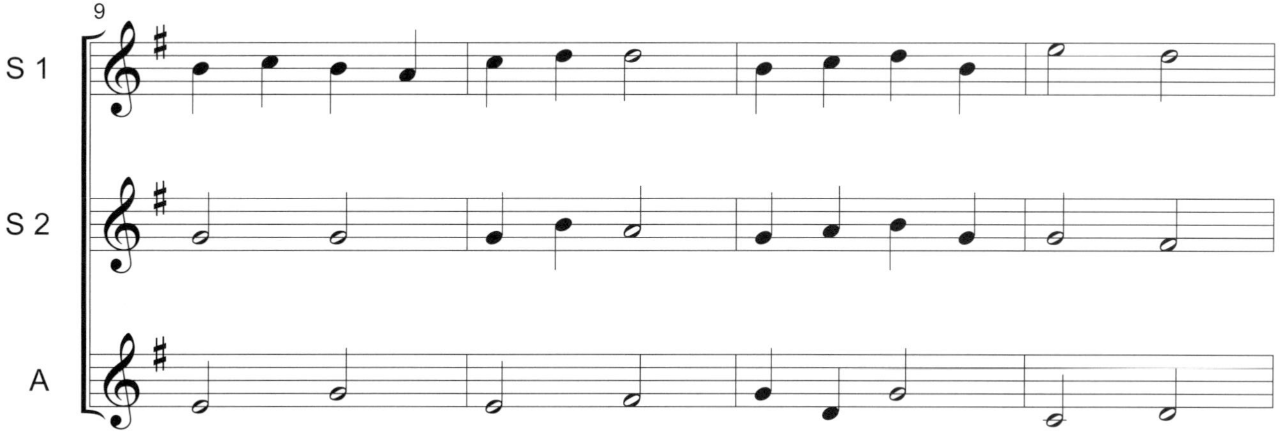
9
S 1
S 2
A

13
S 1
S 2
A

3
Soprano 1
Soprano 2
Alto

5
S 1
S 2
A

9
S 1
S 2
A

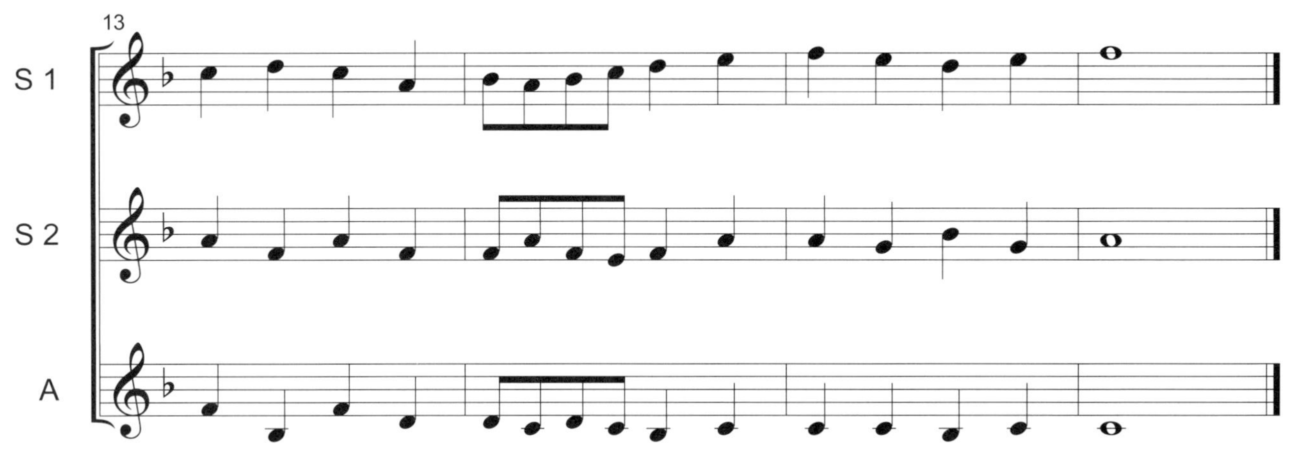
13
S 1
S 2
A

4
Soprano 1
Soprano 2
Alto

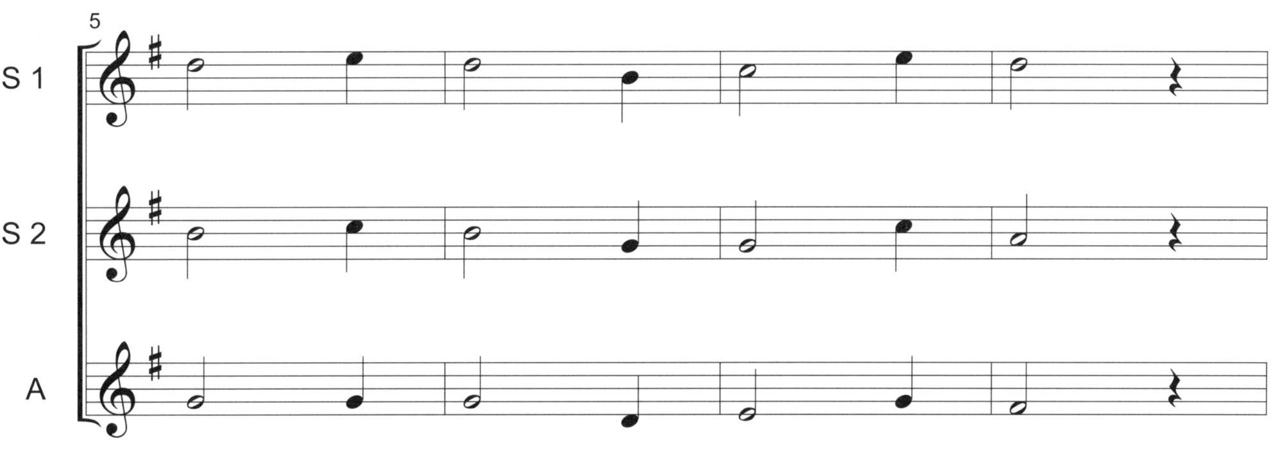
5
S 1
S 2
A

9
S 1
S 2
A

13
S 1
S 2
A

5
Soprano 1
Soprano 2
Alto

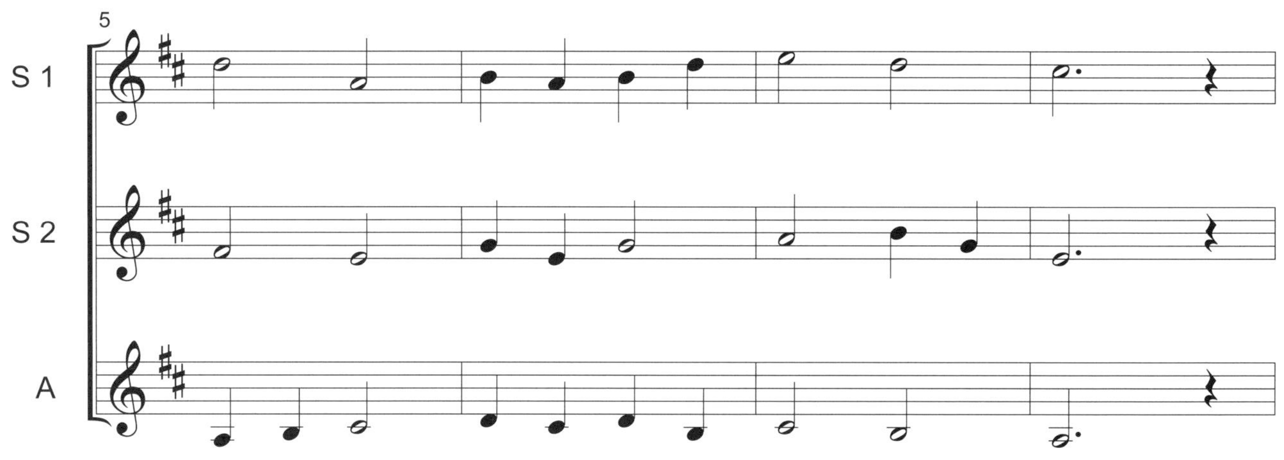
5
S 1
S 2
A

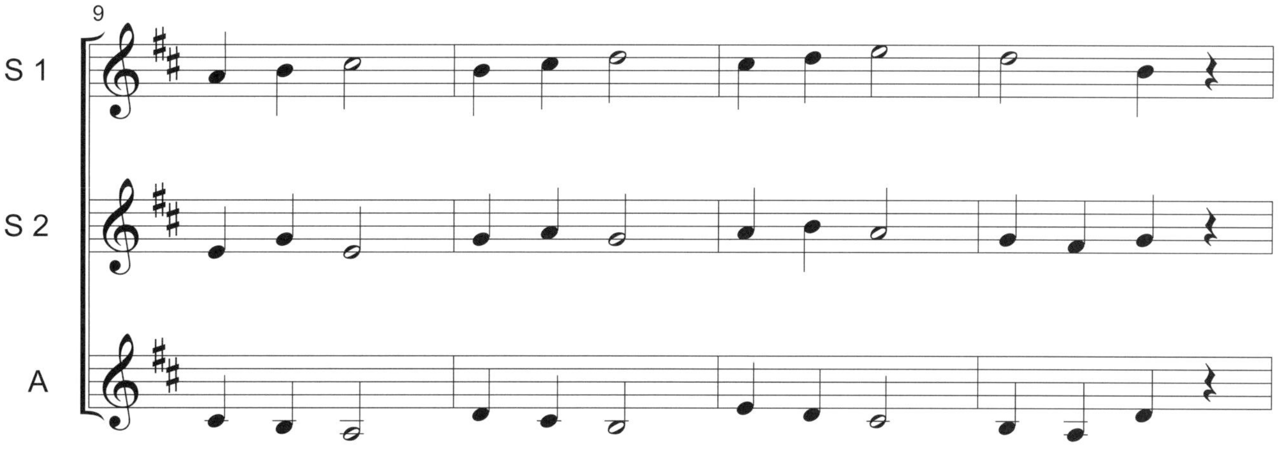
9
S 1
S 2
A

13
S 1
S 2
A

6
Soprano 1
Soprano 2
Alto

5
S 1
S 2
A

9
S 1
S 2
A

13
S 1
S 2
A

7
Soprano 1
Soprano 2
Alto

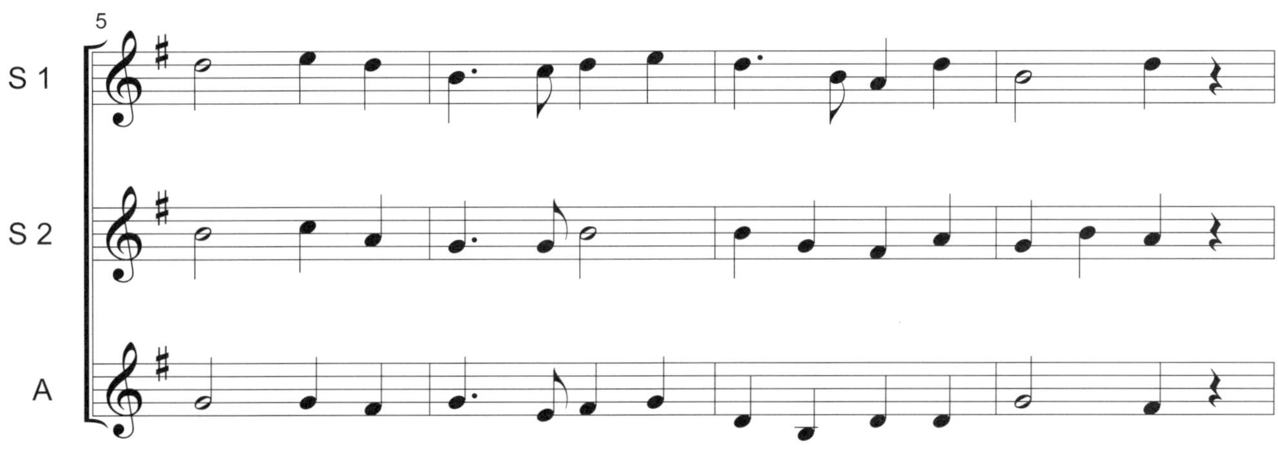
5
S 1
S 2
A

9
S 1
S 2
A

8

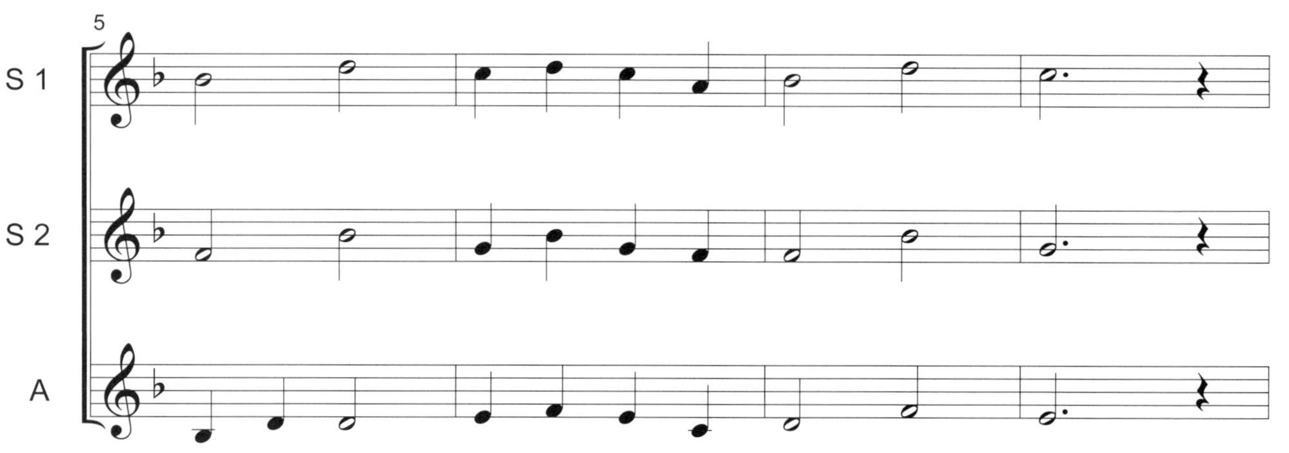

9
S 1
S 2
A

13
S 1
S 2
A

9
Soprano 1
Soprano 2
Alto

5
S 1
S 2
A

9
S 1
S 2
A

13
S 1
S 2
A

10
Soprano 1
Soprano 2
Alto

5
S 1
S 2
A

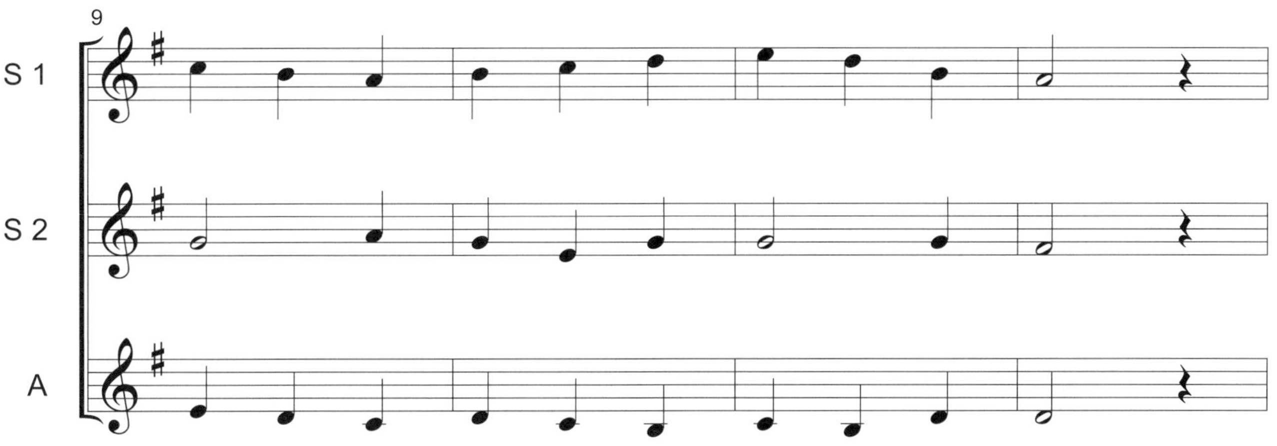
9
S 1
S 2
A

13
S 1
S 2
A

11
Soprano 1
Soprano 2
Alto

5
S 1
S 2
A

9
S 1
S 2
A

13
S 1
S 2
A

12
Soprano 1
Soprano 2
Alto

5
S 1
S 2
A

9
S 1
S 2
A

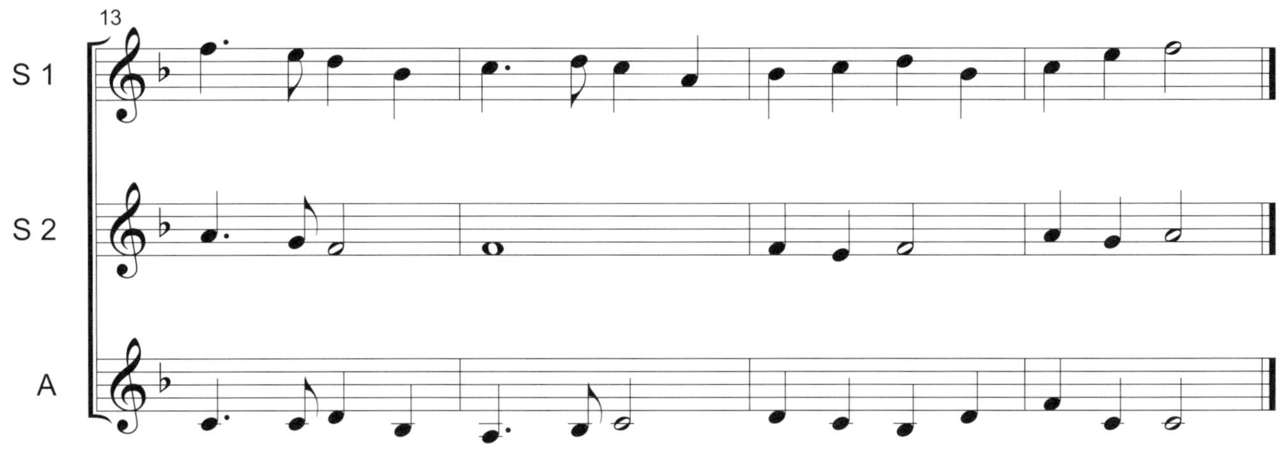
13
S 1
S 2
A

13
Soprano 1
Soprano 2
Alto

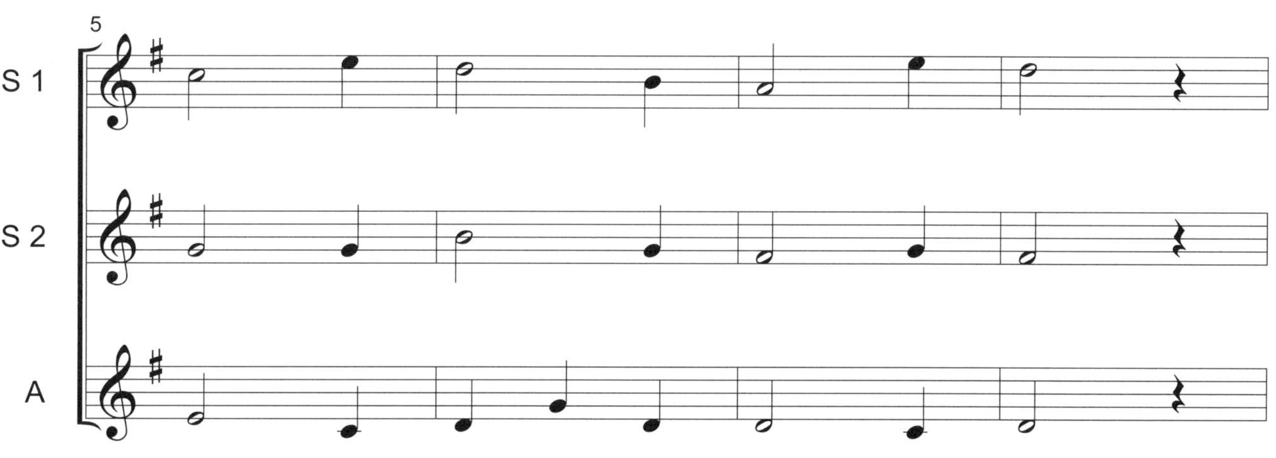
5
S 1
S 2
A

9
S 1
S 2
A

13
S 1
S 2
A
14
Soprano 1
Soprano 2
Alto
5
S 1
S 2
A

9
S 1
S 2
A

13
S 1
S 2
A

15
Soprano 1
Soprano 2
Alto

5
S 1
S 2
A

9
S 1
S 2
A

13
S 1
S 2
A

16
Soprano 1
Soprano 2
Alto

5
S 1
S 2
A

9
S 1
S 2
A

13
S 1
S 2
A

17
Soprano 1
Soprano 2
Alto

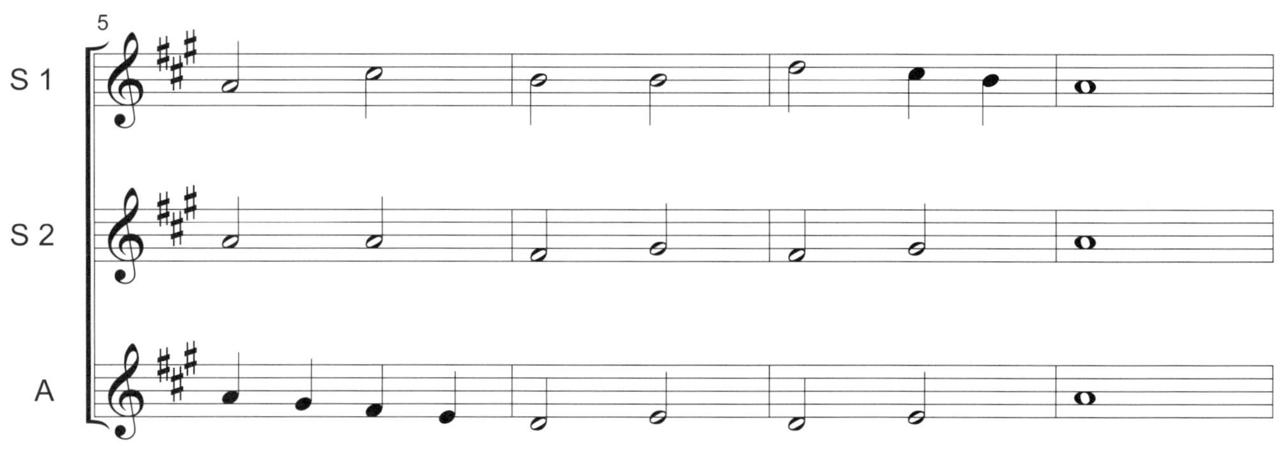
5
S 1
S 2
A

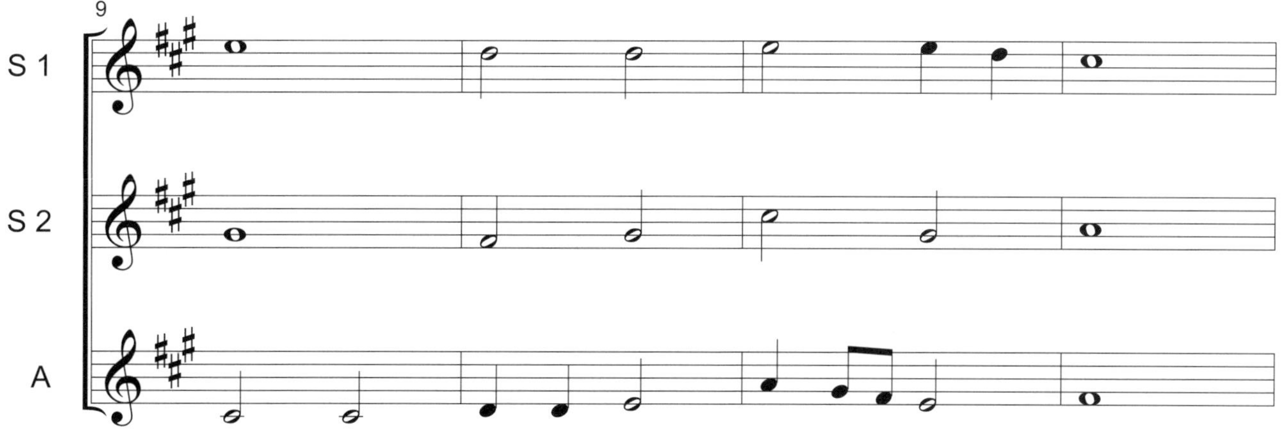
9
S 1
S 2
A

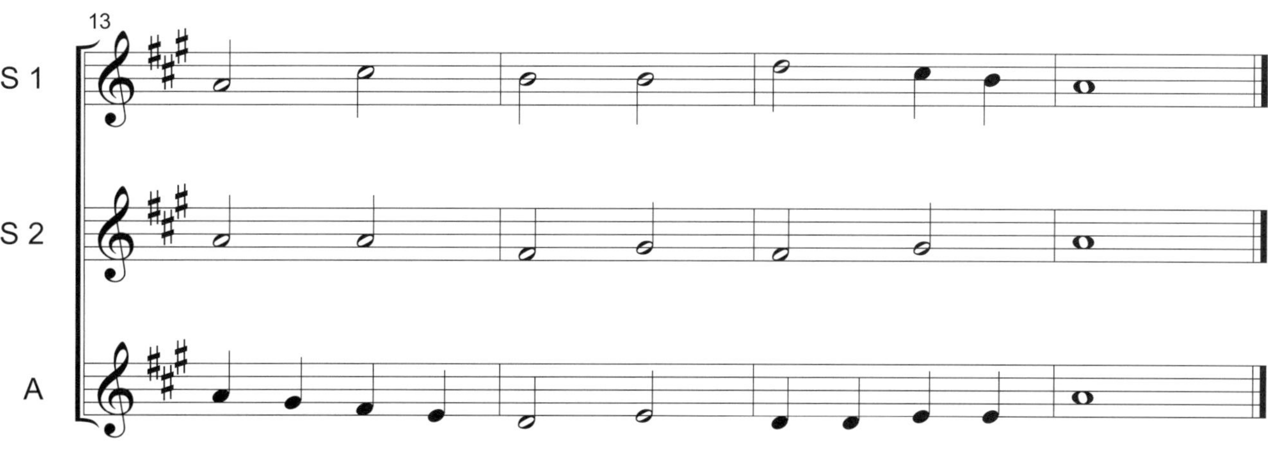
13
S 1
S 2
A

18
Soprano 1
Soprano 2
Alto

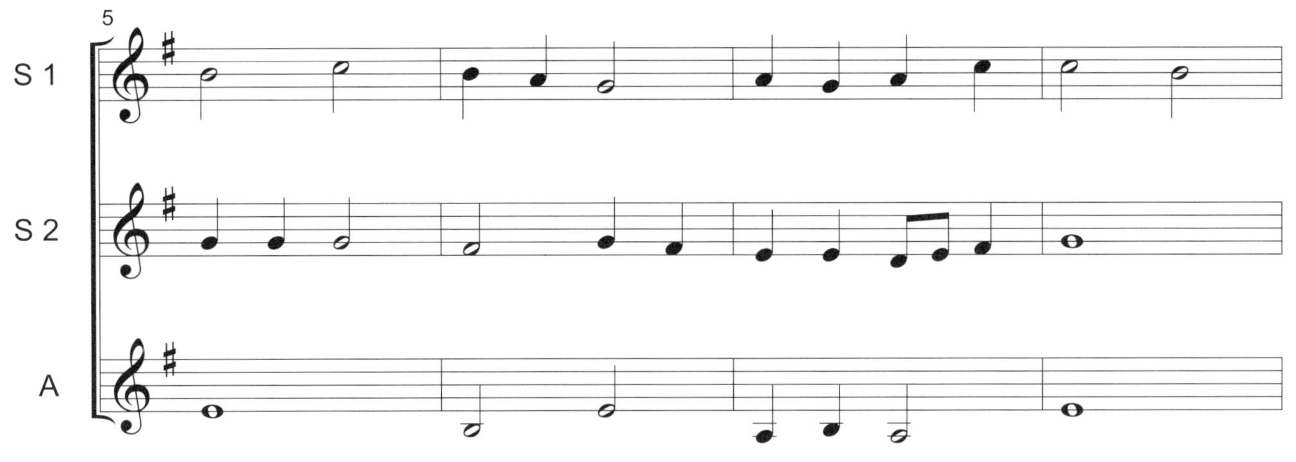
5
S 1
S 2
A

9
S 1
S 2
A

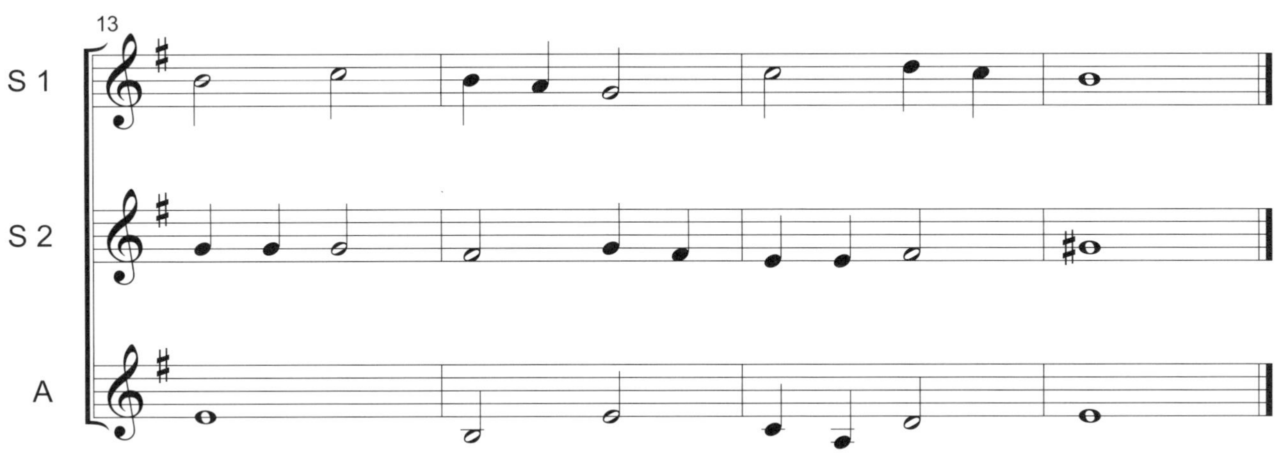
13
S 1
S 2
A

19
Soprano 1
Soprano 2
Alto

5
S 1
S 2
A

9
S 1
S 2
A

13
S 1
S 2
A

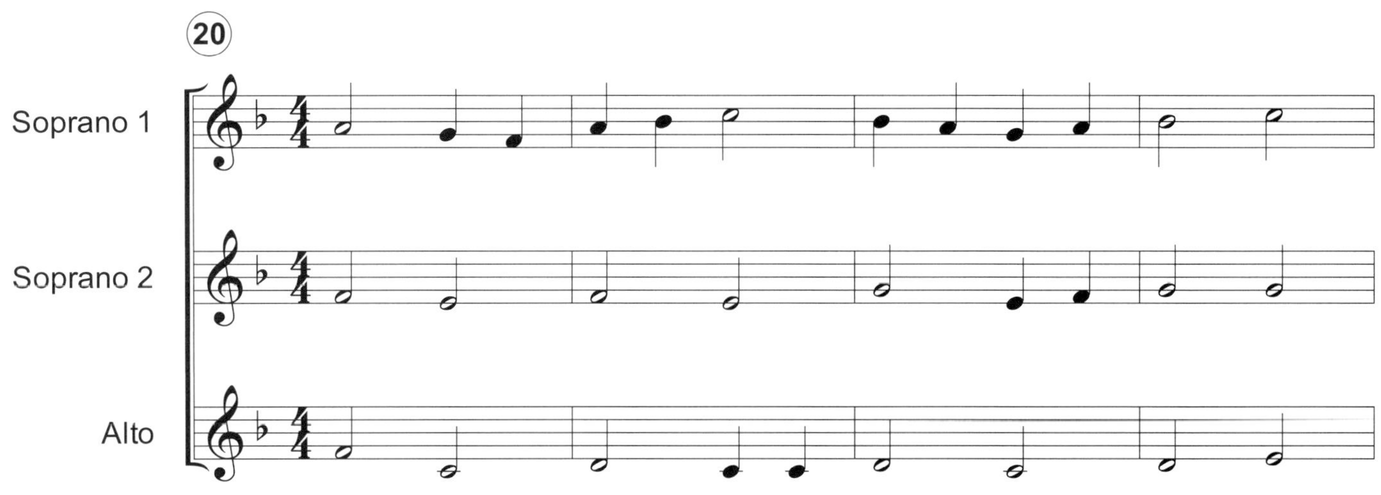
20
Soprano 1
Soprano 2
Alto

5
S 1
S 2
A

9
S 1
S 2
A

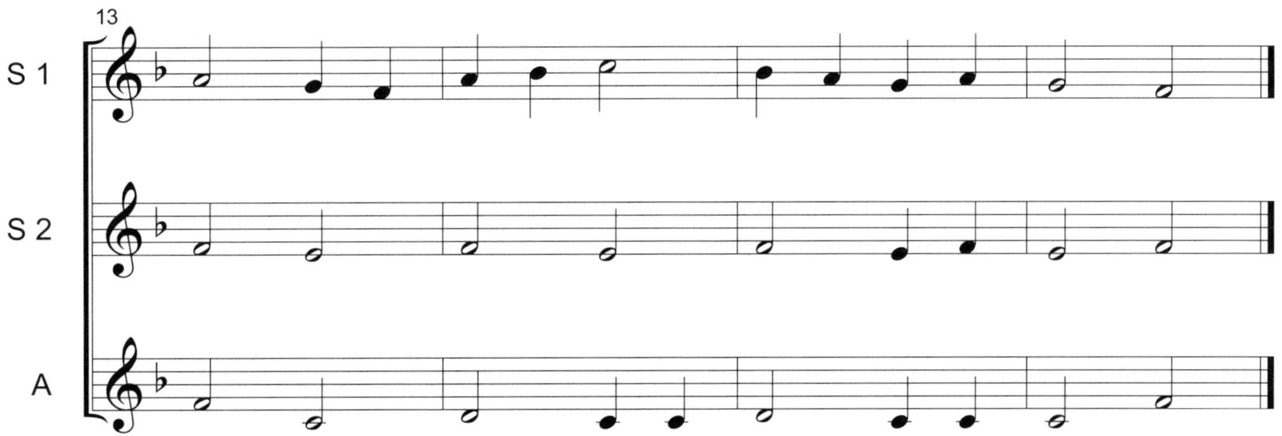
13
S 1
S 2
A

32-MEASURE EXERCISES

13
S 1
S 2
A

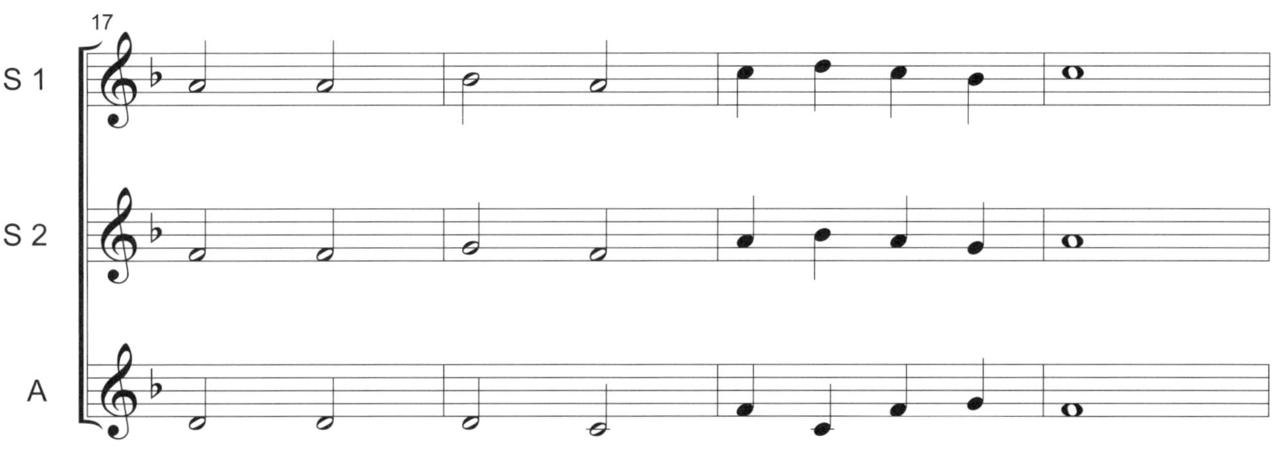
17
S 1
S 2
A

21
S 1
S 2
A

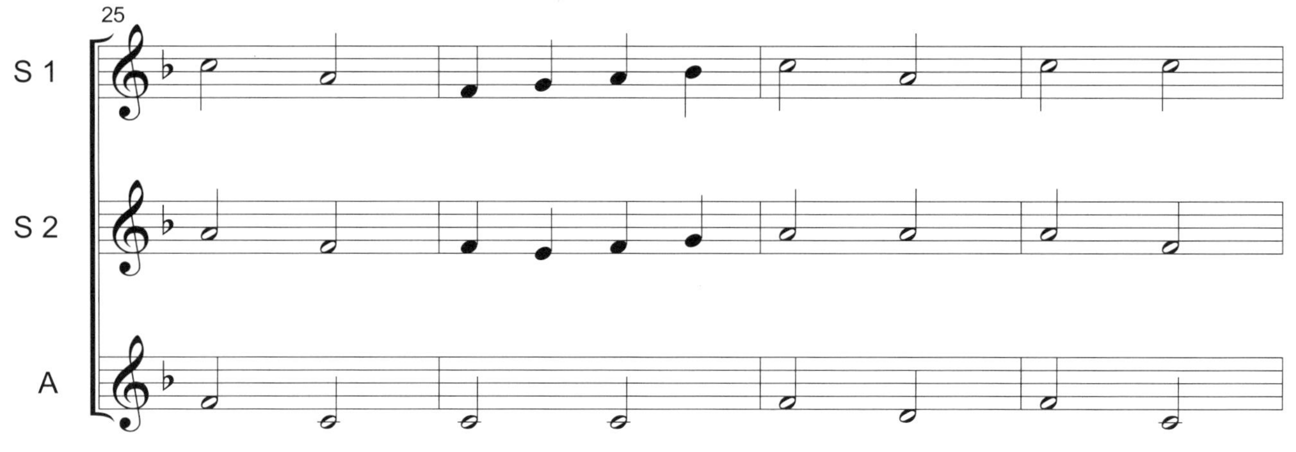
25
S 1
S 2
A

29
S 1
S 2
A

2
Soprano 1
Soprano 2
Alto

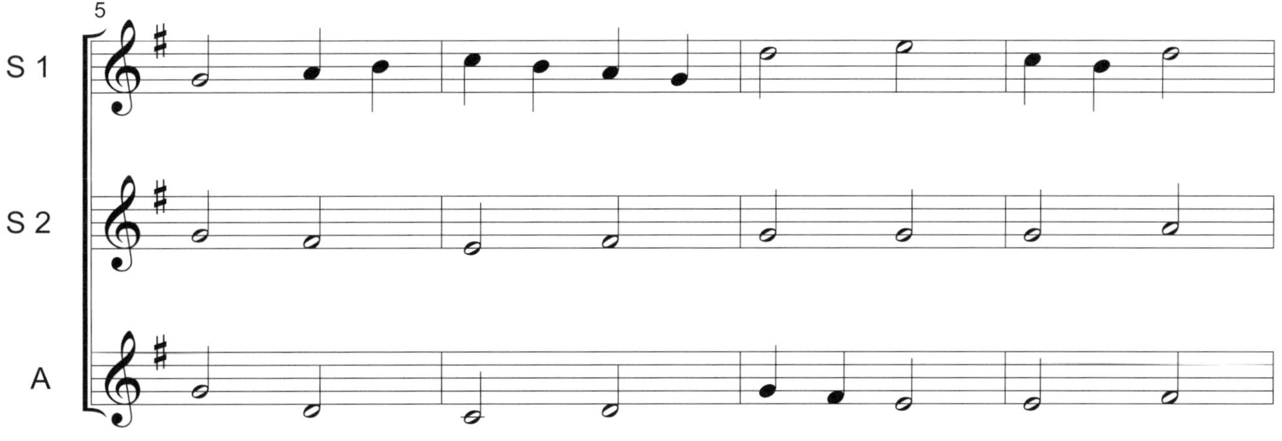
5
S 1
S 2
A

9
S 1
S 2
A

13
S 1
S 2
A

17
S 1
S 2
A

21
S 1
S 2
A

25
S 1
S 2
A

29
S 1
S 2
A

3
Soprano 1
Soprano 2
Alto

5
S 1
S 2
A

9
S 1
S 2
A

13
S 1
S 2
A

17
S 1
S 2
A

21
S 1
S 2
A

25
S 1
S 2
A

29
S 1
S 2
A

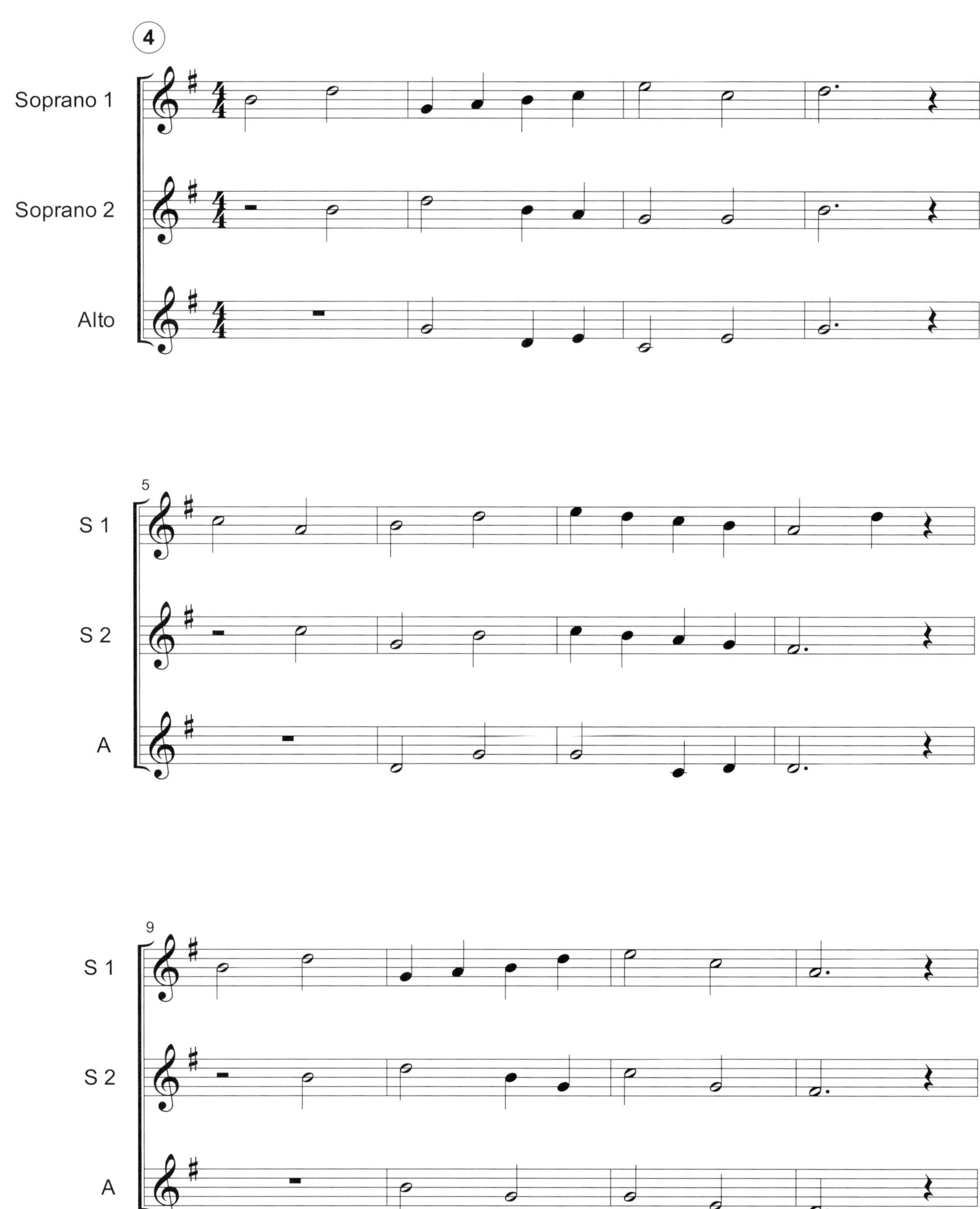
4
Soprano 1
Soprano 2
Alto
5
S 1
S 2
A
9
S 1
S 2
A

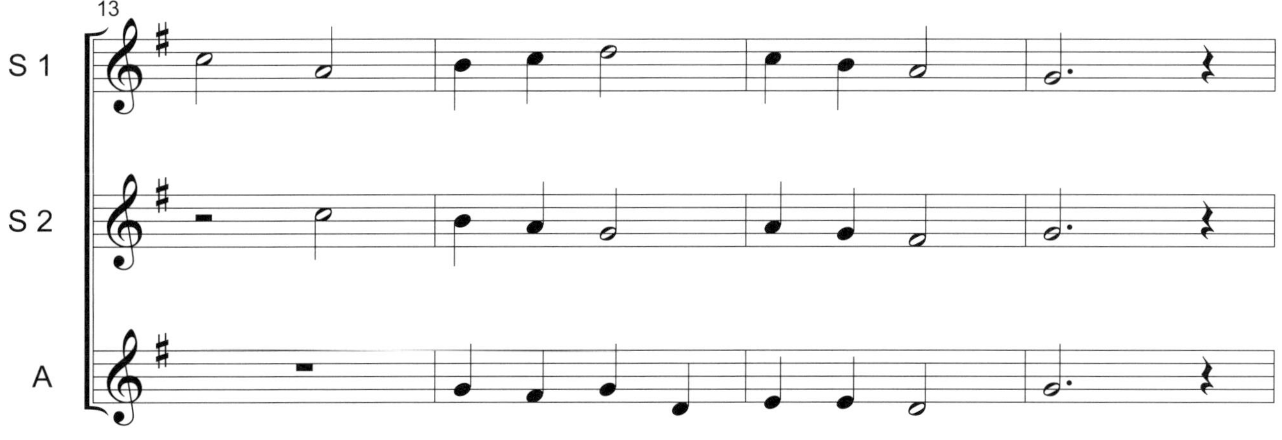
13
S 1
S 2
A

17
S 1
S 2
A

21
S 1
S 2
A

25
S 1
S 2
A

29
S 1
S 2
A

5
Soprano 1
Soprano 2
Alto

5
S 1
S 2
A

9
S 1
S 2
A

13
S 1
S 2
A

17
S 1
S 2
A

21
S 1
S 2
A

25
S 1
S 2
A

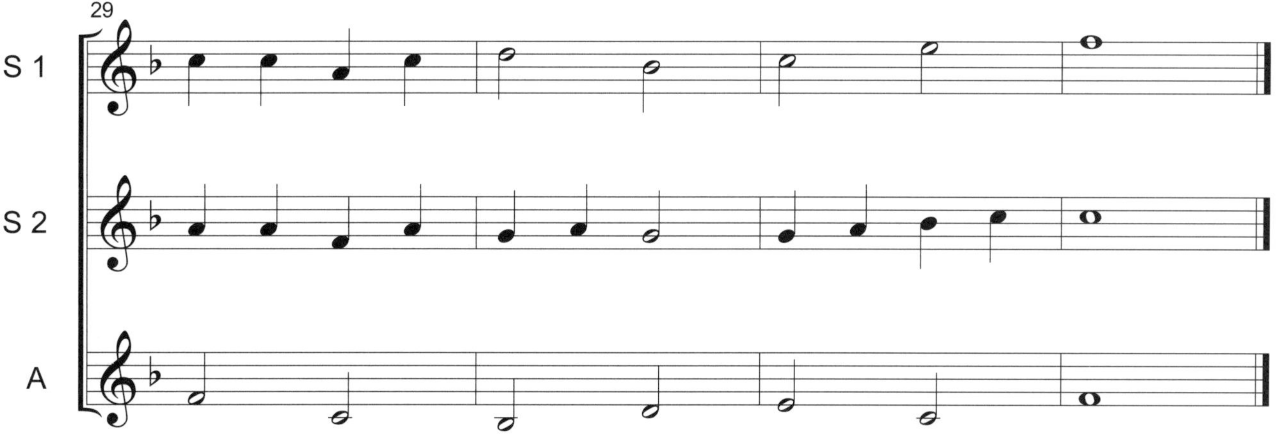
29
S 1
S 2
A

6
Soprano 1
Soprano 2
Alto

5
S 1
S 2
A

9
S 1
S 2
A

13
S 1
S 2
A

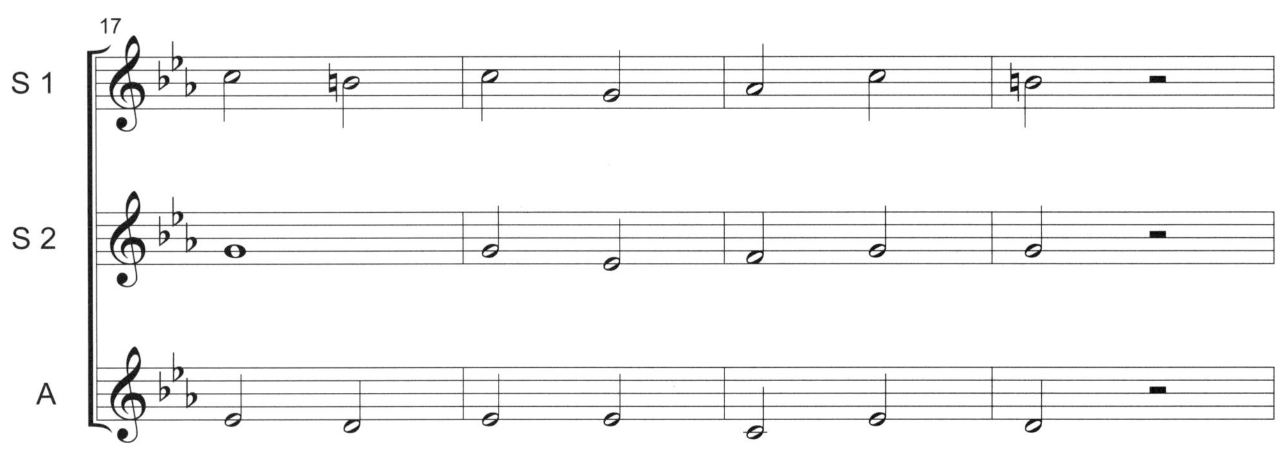
17
S 1
S 2
A

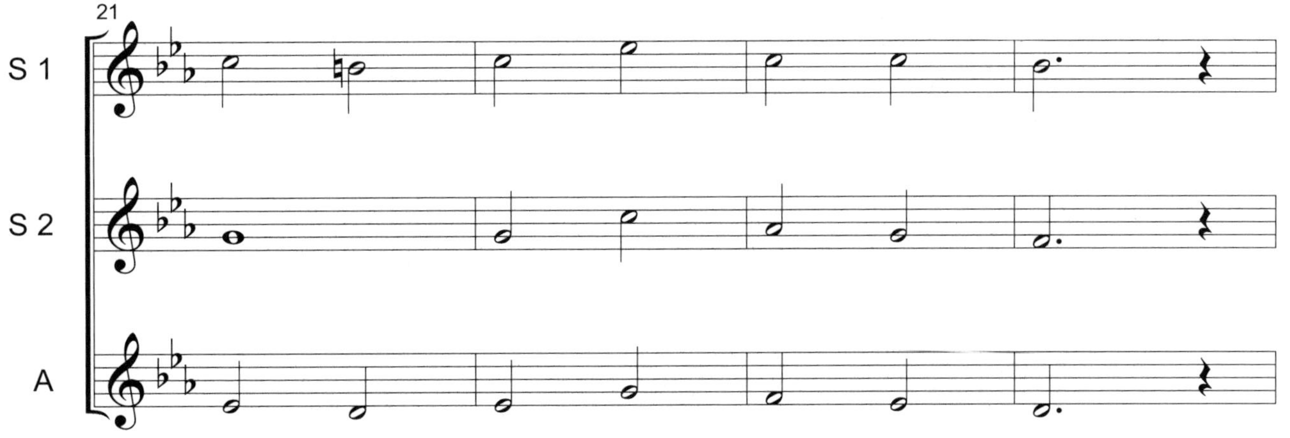
21
S 1
S 2
A

25
S 1
S 2
A

29
S 1
S 2
A

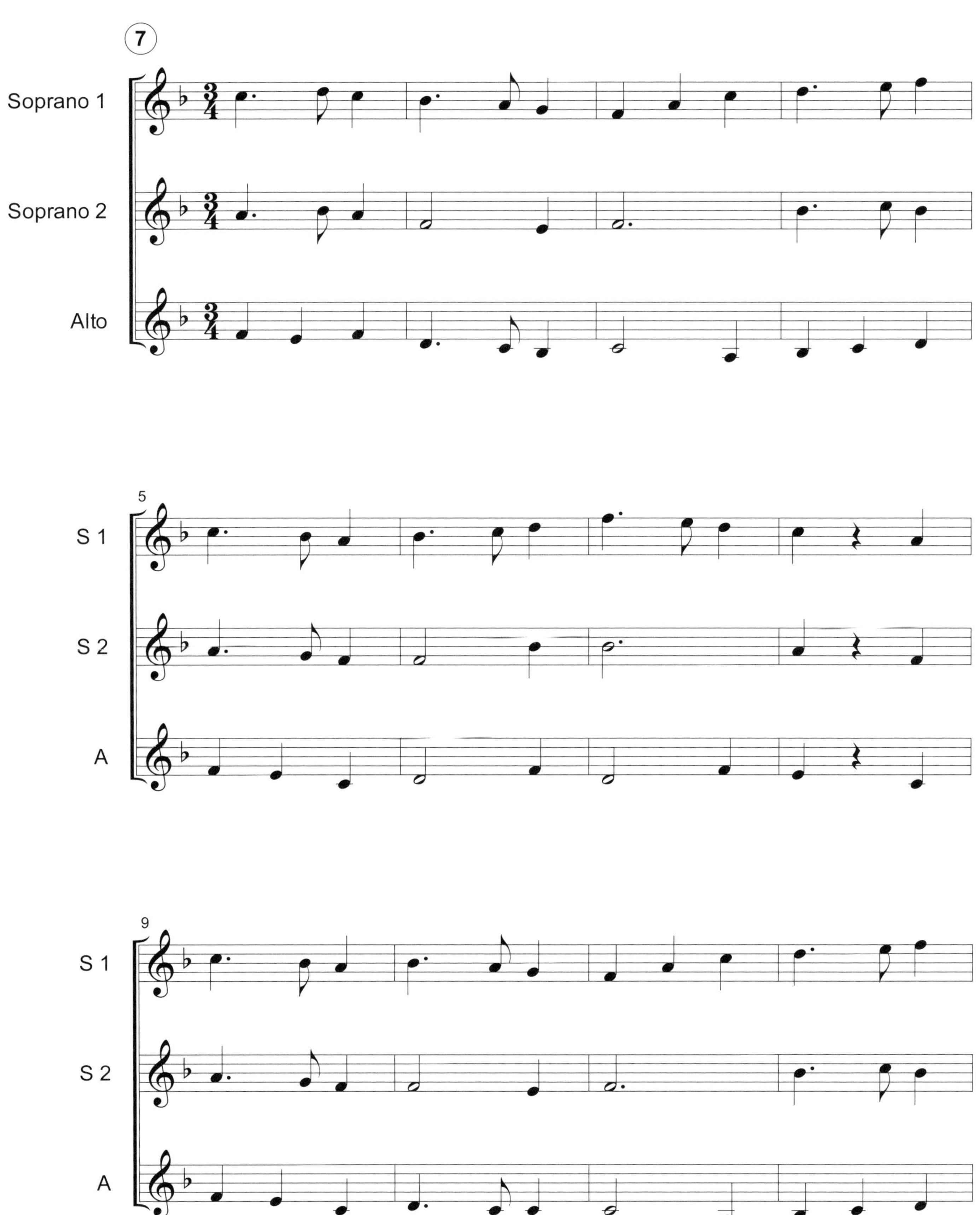
7
Soprano 1
Soprano 2
Alto
5
S 1
S 2
A
9
S 1
S 2
A

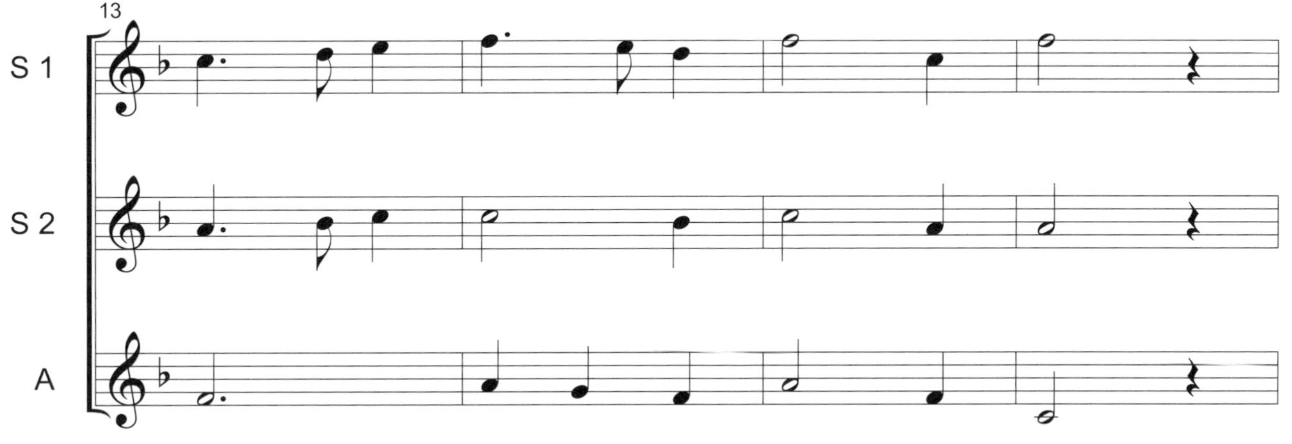
13
S 1
S 2
A

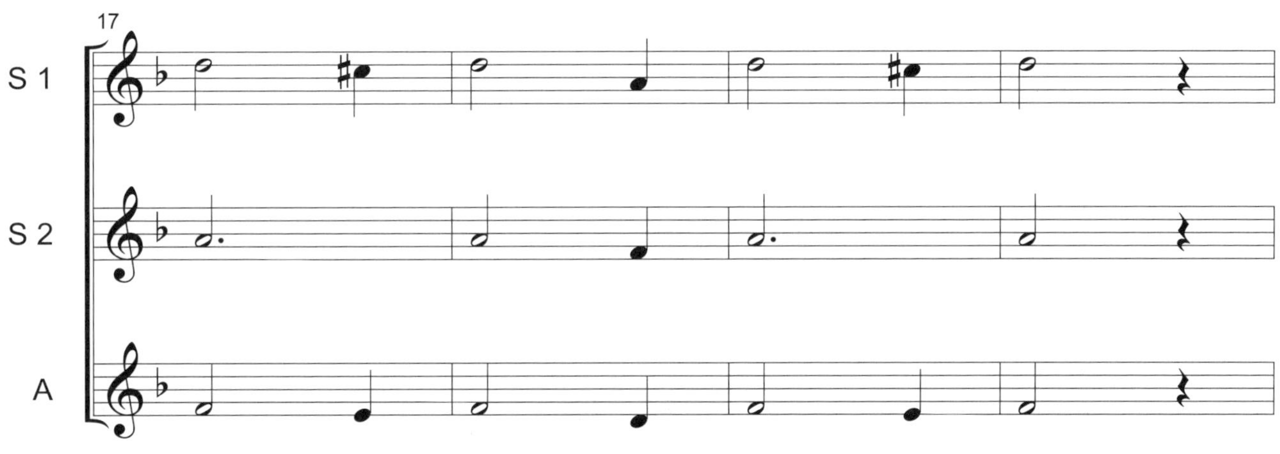
17
S 1
S 2
A

21
S 1
S 2
A

25
S 1
S 2
A

29
S 1
S 2
A

8
Soprano 1
Soprano 2
Alto

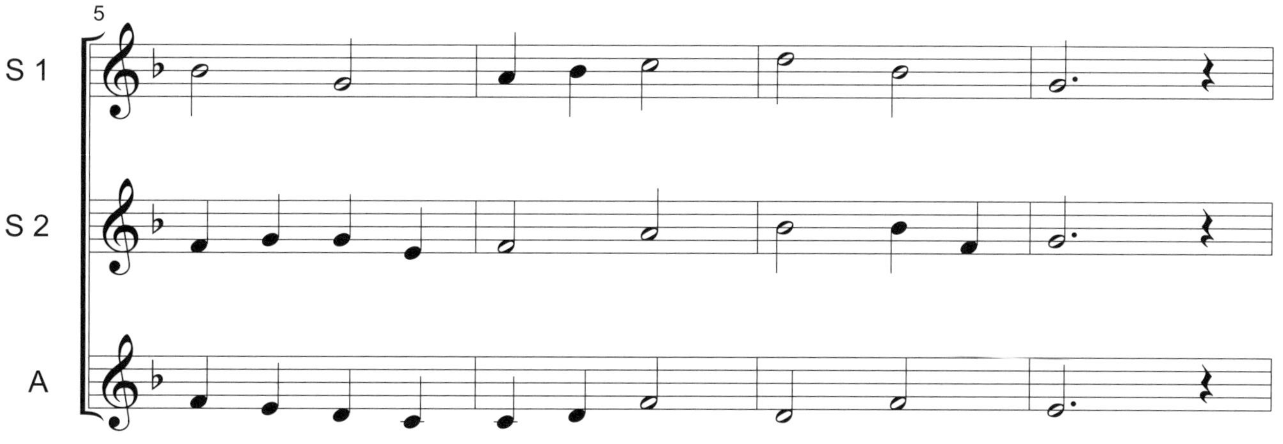
5
S 1
S 2
A

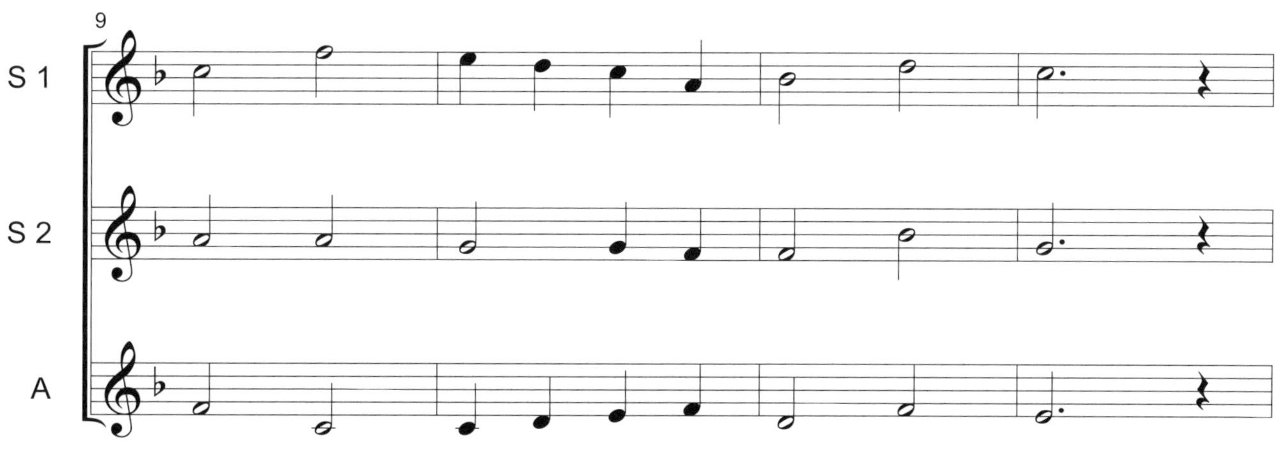
9
S 1
S 2
A

13
S 1
S 2
A

17
S 1
S 2
A

21
S 1
S 2
A

25
S 1
S 2
A

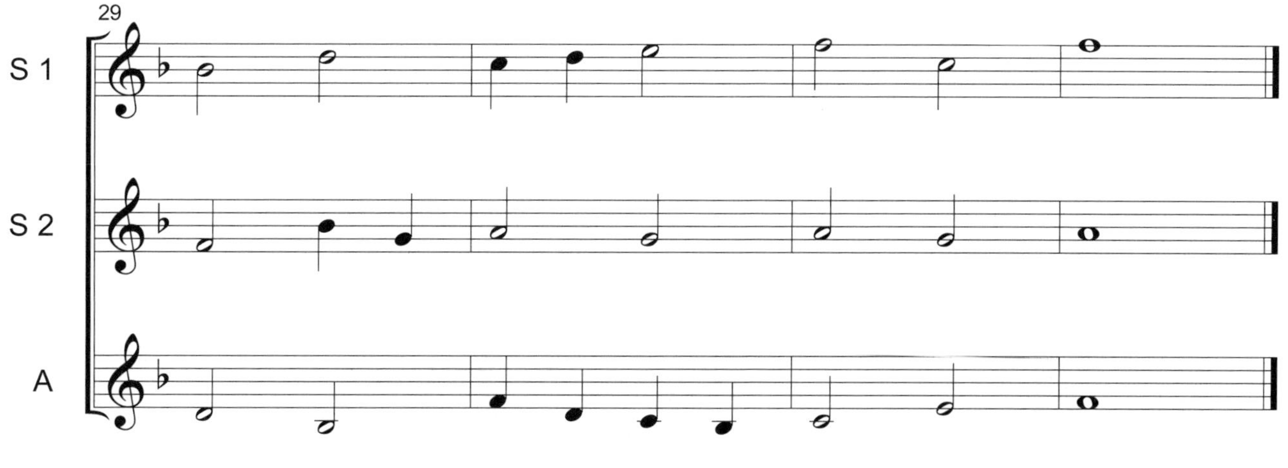
29
S 1
S 2
A

9
Soprano 1
Soprano 2
Alto

5
S 1
S 2
A

9
S 1
S 2
A

13
S 1
S 2
A

17
S 1
S 2
A

21
S 1
S 2
A

25
S 1
S 2
A

29
S 1
S 2
A

10
Soprano 1
Soprano 2
Alto

5
S 1
S 2
A

9
S 1
S 2
A

13
S 1
S 2
A

17
S 1
S 2
A

21
S 1
S 2
A

25
S 1
S 2
A

29
S 1
S 2
A

11
Soprano 1
Soprano 2
Alto

5
S 1
S 2
A

9
S 1
S 2
A

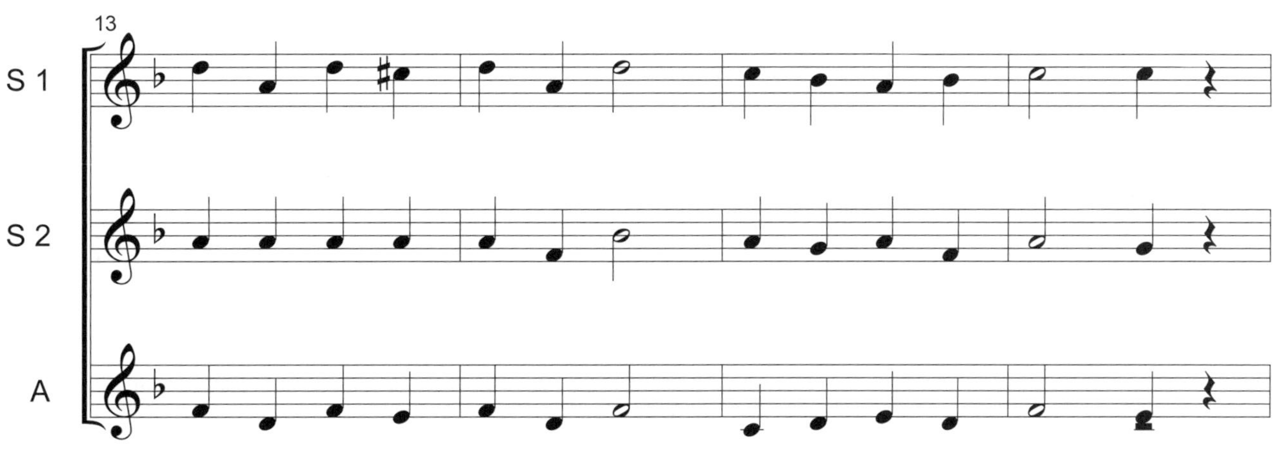
13
S 1
S 2
A

17
S 1
S 2
A

21
S 1
S 2
A

25
S 1
S 2
A

29
S 1
S 2
A

12
Soprano 1
Soprano 2
Alto

5
S 1
S 2
A

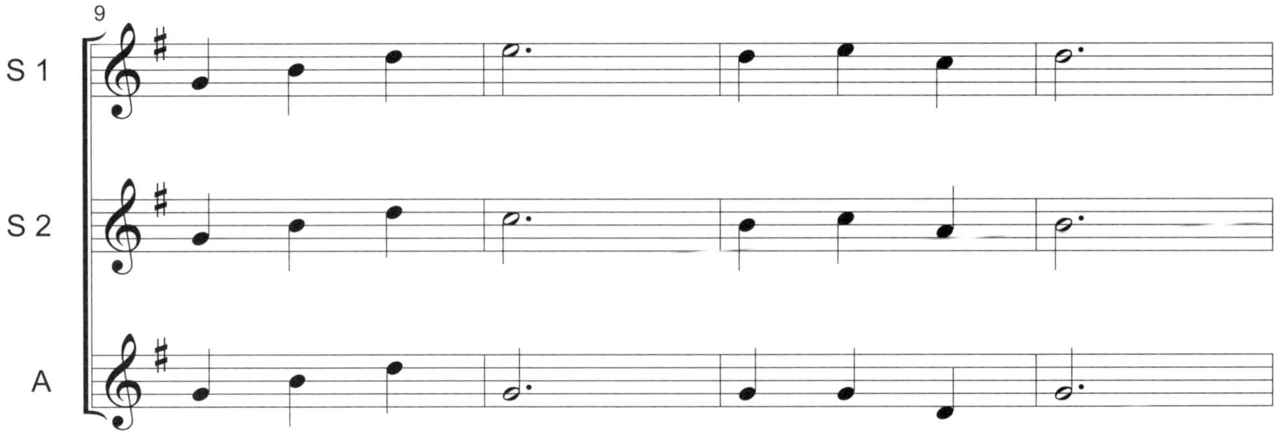

9

S 1

S 2

A

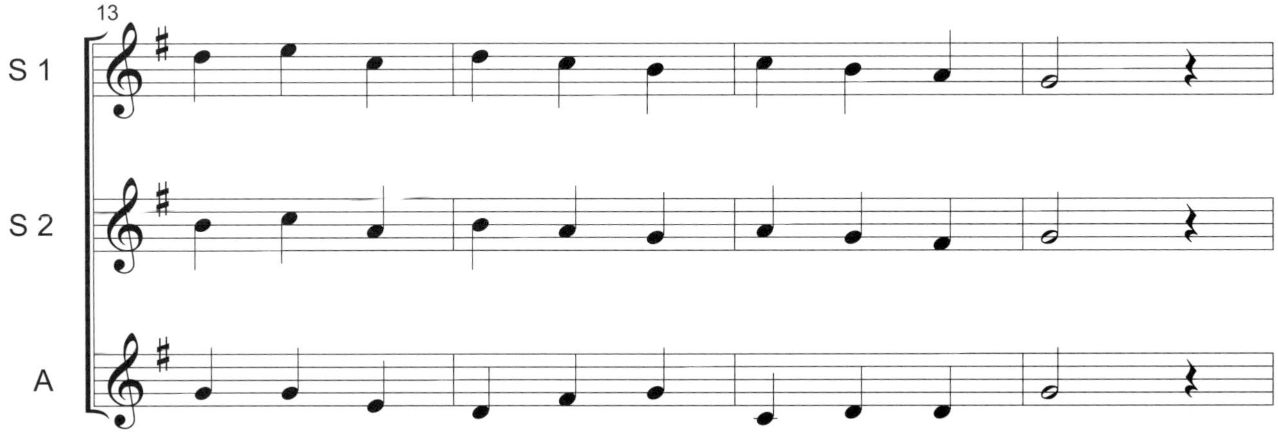

13

S 1

S 2

A

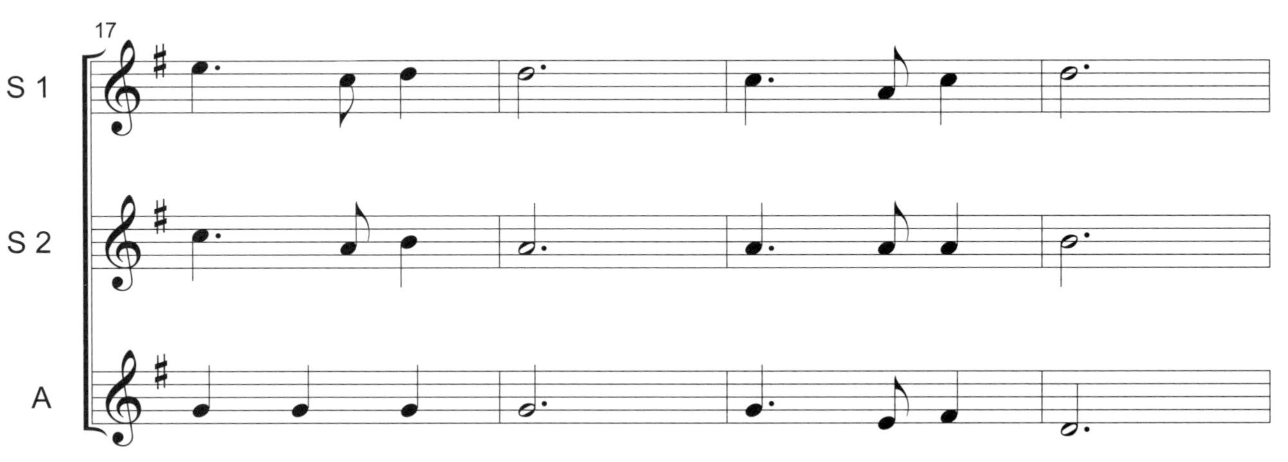

21
S 1
S 2
A

25
S 1
S 2
A

29
S 1
S 2
A

13
Soprano 1
Soprano 2
Alto
5
S 1
S 2
A
9
S 1
S 2
A

13
S 1
S 2
A

17
S 1
S 2
A

21
S 1
S 2
A

25
S 1
S 2
A

29
S 1
S 2
A

14
Soprano 1
Soprano 2
Alto

5
S 1
S 2
A

9
S 1
S 2
A

13
S 1
S 2
A

17
S 1
S 2
A

21
S 1
S 2
A

25
S 1
S 2
A

29
S 1
S 2
A

15
Soprano 1
Soprano 2
Alto

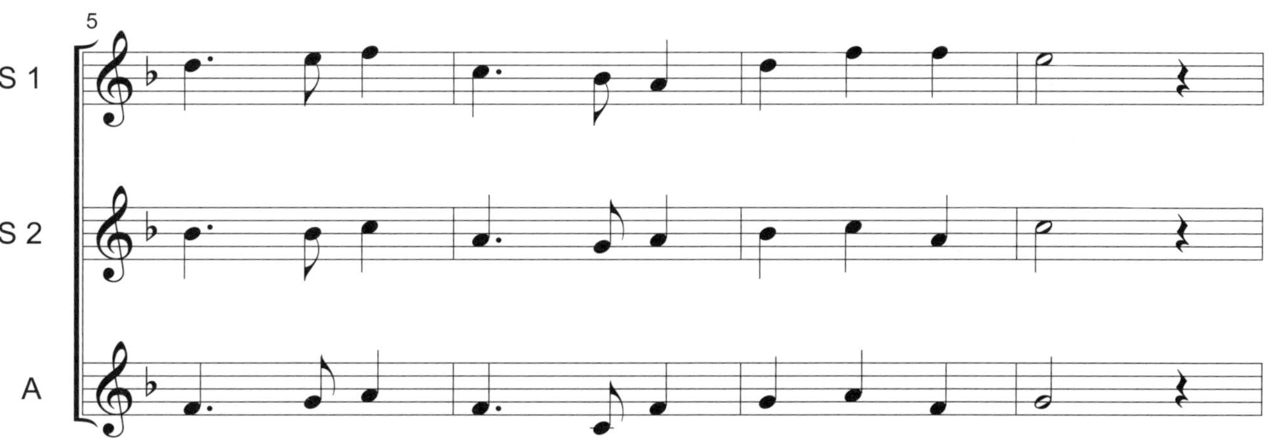
5
S 1
S 2
A

9
S 1
S 2
A

13
S 1
S 2
A

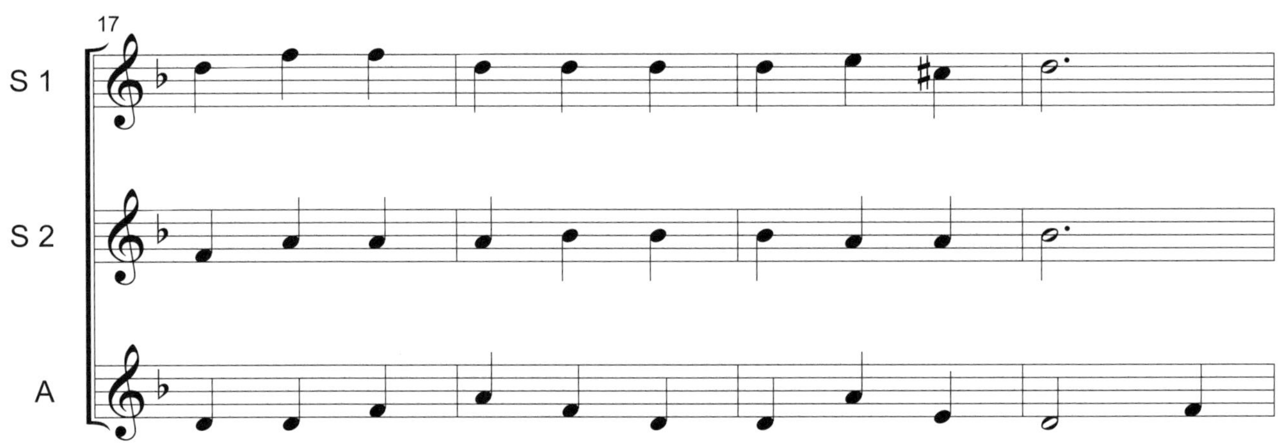
17
S 1
S 2
A

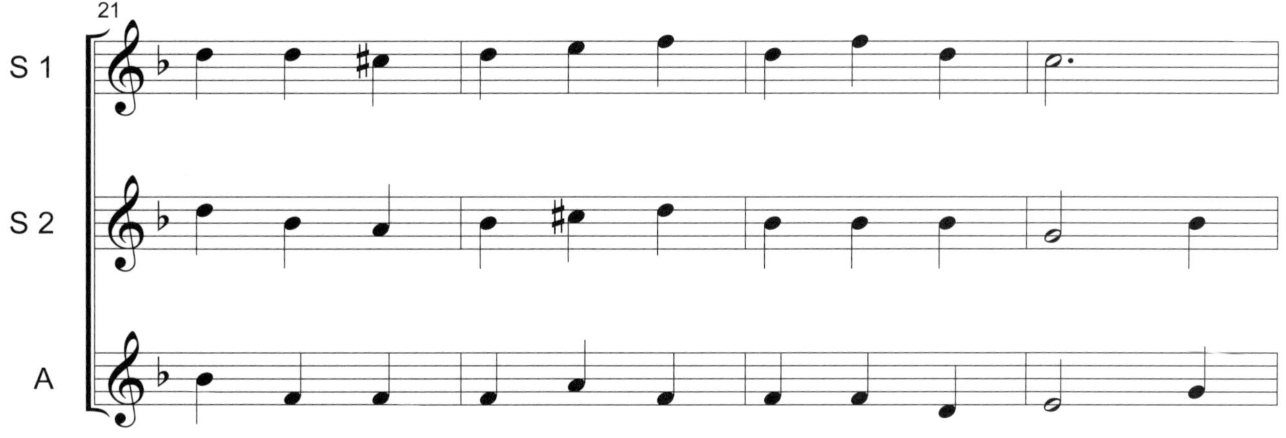
21
S 1
S 2
A

25
S 1
S 2
A

29
S 1
S 2
A

16
Soprano 1
Soprano 2
Alto
5
S 1
S 2
A
9
S 1
S 2
A

13
S 1
S 2
A

17
S 1
S 2
A

21
S 1
S 2
A

25
S 1
S 2
A

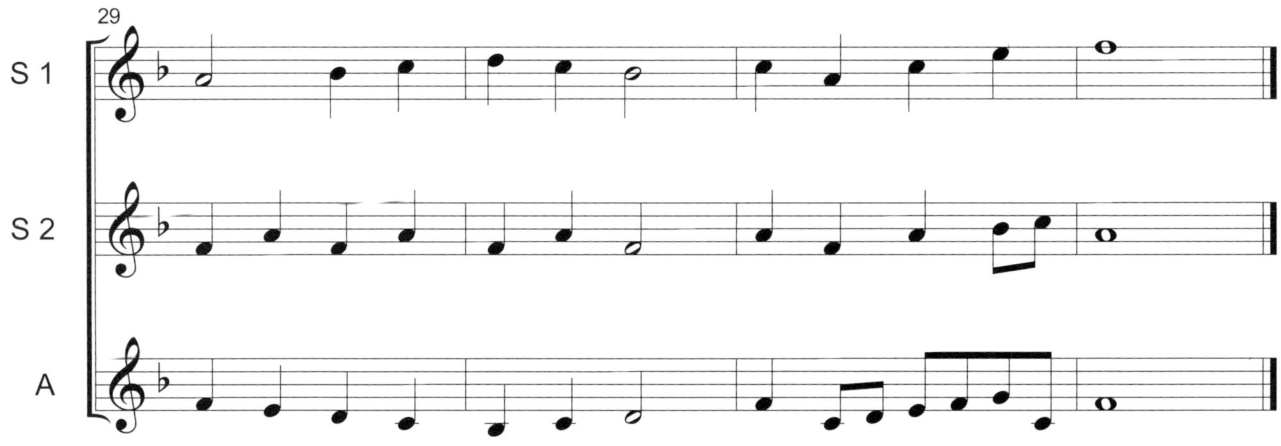
29
S 1
S 2
A

17
Soprano 1
Soprano 2
Alto

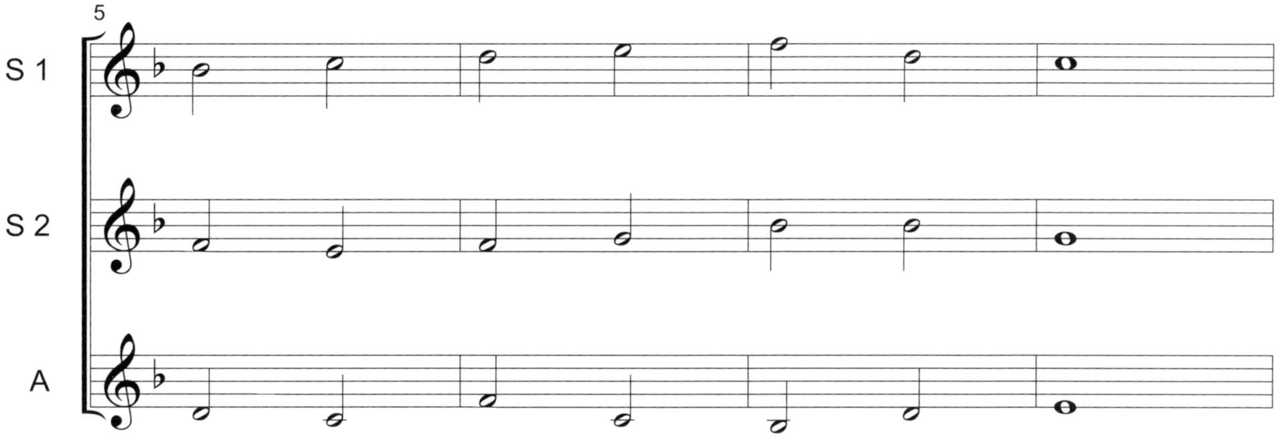
5
S 1
S 2
A

9
S 1
S 2
A

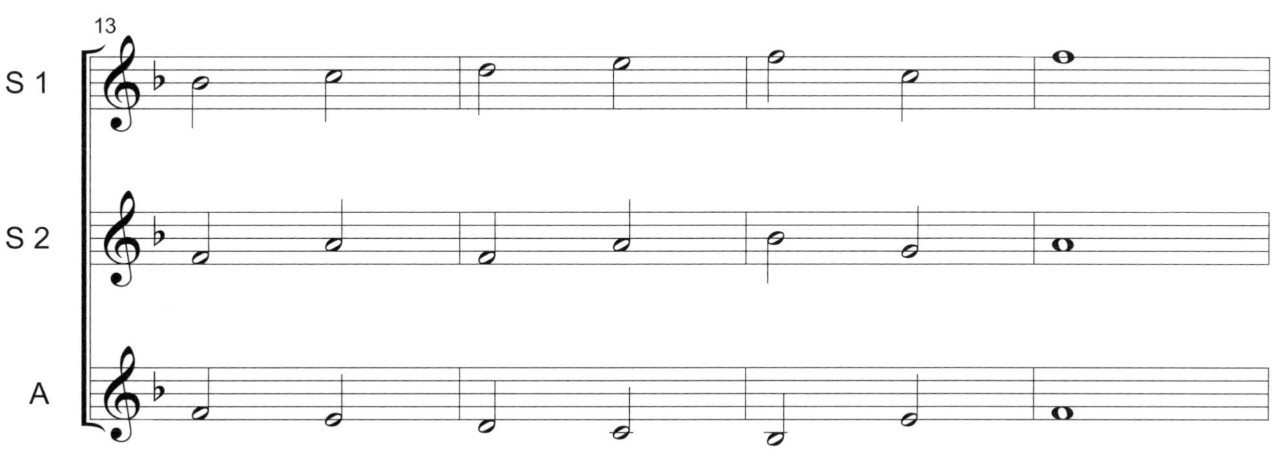
13
S 1
S 2
A

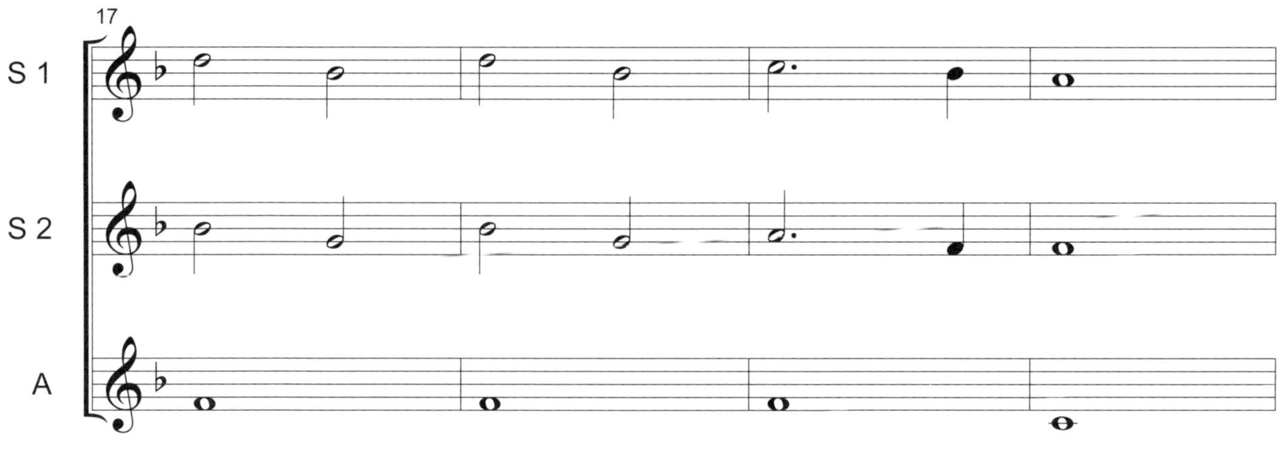
17
S 1
S 2
A

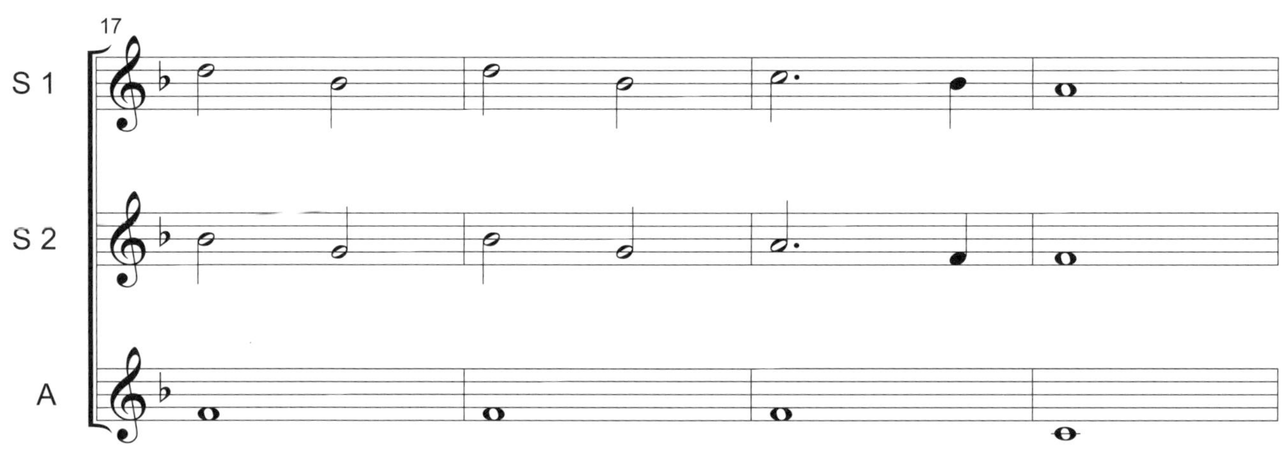
17
S 1
S 2
A

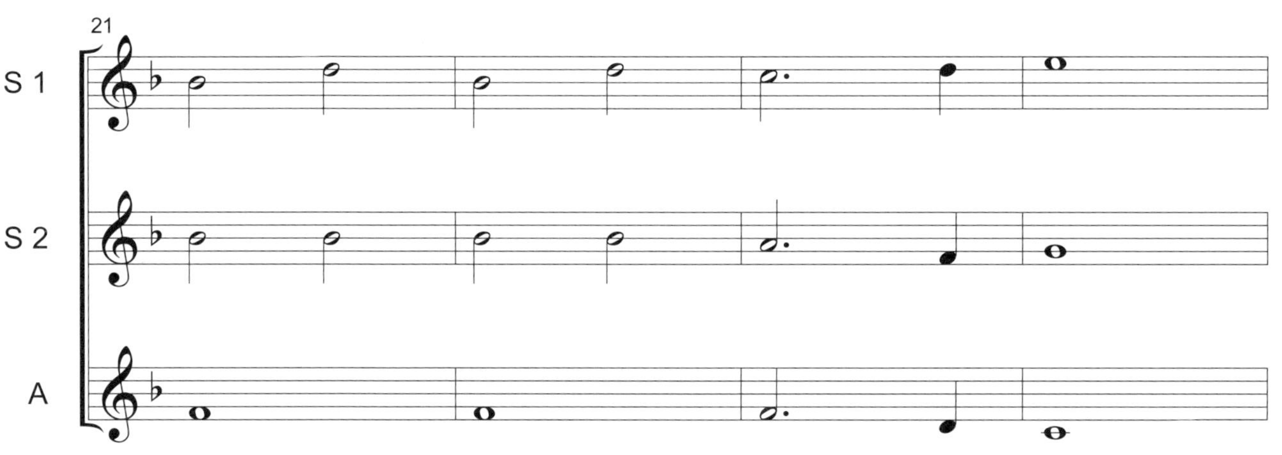
21
S 1
S 2
A

29
S 1
S 2
A

18
Soprano 1
Soprano 2
Alto

5
S 1
S 2
A

9
S 1
S 2
A

13
S 1
S 2
A

17
S 1
S 2
A

21
S 1
S 2
A

25
S 1
S 2
A

29
S 1
S 2
A

19
Soprano 1
Soprano 2
Alto
5
S 1
S 2
A
9
S 1
S 2
A

13
S 1
S 2
A

17
S 1
S 2
A

21
S 1
S 2
A

25
S 1
S 2
A

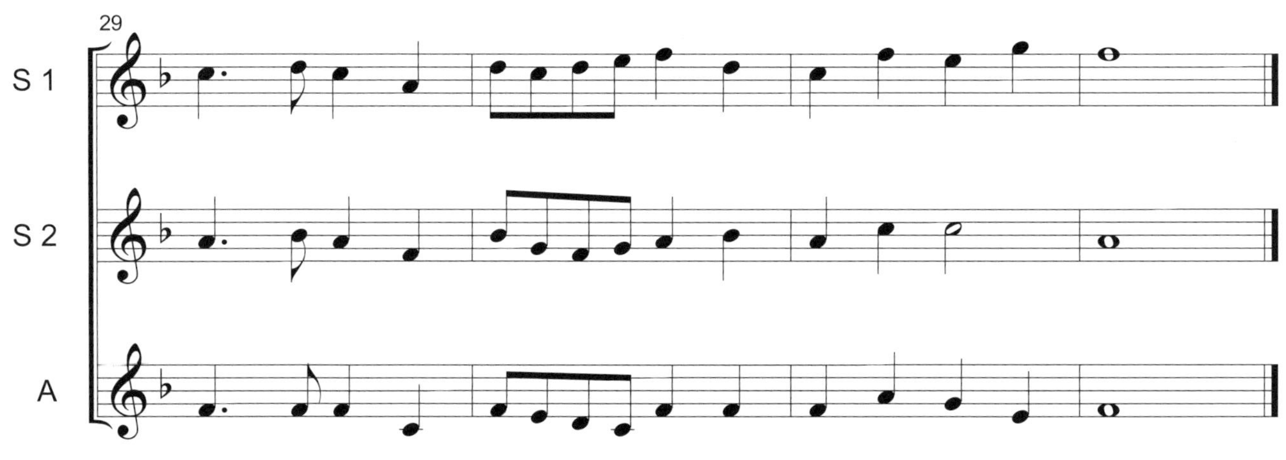
29
S 1
S 2
A

20
Soprano 1
Soprano 2
Alto

5
S 1
S 2
A

9
S 1
S 2
A

13
S 1
S 2
A

17
S 1
S 2
A

21
S 1
S 2
A

25
S 1
S 2
A

29
S 1
S 2
A

ABOUT THE AUTHORS

H. Morris Stevens, Jr. Ph.D. is currently Assistant Professor, and Head of the Music Department at St. Edward's University in Austin, Texas. From 1989 until 2007 he was head choral director, and co-founder of the Fine Arts Academy at Westwood High School in Round Rock, Texas. Prior to that Dr. Stevens was head director at McCallum High School in Austin, Texas for ten years, and head director at John Jay High School in San Antonio, Texas for four years. He is a strong advocate for commissioning and premiering new choral works from more than twenty composers.

He often serves as an adjudicator and clinician for choral contests and festivals across the country and is proud to be Associate Music Minister at St. Theresa's Catholic Church in Austin since 1981.

Dr. Stevens received his bachelor's degree from the University of Texas at Austin and his master's degree in choral conducting from the University of Texas at San Antonio. He completed the Ph.D. in Music Education from the University of Texas at Austin in 2001. Morris is very grateful for his wife Polly. Their greatest treasured times are spent with three grown children, Sarah, Patrick and Rebekah, their spouses, and grandchildren.

Stan McGill taught 33 years in secondary choral music education in Texas and Missouri. He concluded his teaching tenure in 2008 at Highland Park High School in Dallas after serving as the head choral director at South Garland High School, Garland, Texas for 24 years. Professional positions include Texas Music Educators Association Vocal Chair and President of both TMEA and Southwest American Choral Directors Association. He has served on numerous TMEA, TCDA, SWACDA and ACDA committees including Program and Site Chair for several National ACDA and SWACDA Conferences. He is active as an adjudicator, speaker, director and clinician throughout the United States. In 2014 he received the TCDA Choral Excellence Award given for Mr. McGill's contributions to choral music in Texas, mentorship and inspiration to colleagues and students, and continued advocacy for the future of choral singing.

Mr. McGill's articles have been published in the Southwestern Musician, Common Times, Choral Journal, and Texas Sings. He has directed numerous honor choirs including all-state choirs in Alaska, Arkansas, Connecticut, Kentucky, New Mexico, Oklahoma, and South Carolina as well as ACDA Honor Choirs. His choirs performed a total of nine times for TMEA, SWACDA and National ACDA Conventions. A native of Sikeston, Missouri, Mr. McGill received his undergraduate degree from William Jewell College and his MME from Arizona State University.